Sex, with Love

Sex, with Love

A Guide for Young People

Eleanor Hamilton, Ph.D.

BEACON PRESS · Boston

Copyright © 1978 by Eleanor Hamilton, Ph.D.

Beacon Press books are published under the auspices
of the Unitarian Universalist Association

Published simultaneously in Canada by
Fitzhenry & Whiteside Limited, Toronto

Printed in the United States of America

(hardcover) 9 8 7 6 5 4 3 2 1
(paperback) 9 8 7 6 5 4 3

Library of Congress Cataloging in Publication Data

Hamilton, Eleanor, 1909—
     Sex, with love.
     Bibliography: p.
     Includes index.
     1. Sex instruction for youth.   I. Title.
HQ35.H343   613.9'5   77—75442
ISBN 0—8070—2580—1
ISBN 0—8070—2581—X (pbk.)

Contents

Introduction

The word *sex*, when coupled with the word *love*, makes the most exciting phrase in our language. For sexual love is a power source that makes life worth living. It is also what makes life go on.

It generates the energy for the accomplishment of great deeds, for overcoming otherwise impossible obstacles, for the solution of difficult problems.

Because of sexual love, human beings seek each other for comfort, for pleasure, for companionship, for inspiration, and because they wish to have babies.

It is precisely because sexuality is such an important potential source for good in your life that it will reward you to know as much as you possibly can about it—how it works, and how to make it work positively for you.

Sex, with Love

1 Growth

Breasts, Beards, Acne

Most adults tend to commiserate with adolescents over the trials and tribulations of growing up. They really needn't. Perhaps they are still reeling from the speed of it, or perhaps they grew up too soon and leveled off to nongrowth. But make no mistake about it, you are in for *fun* as you move forward into the wonderful topsy-turvy time of puberty.

Growing, in fact, is one of the rewarding adventures of life. The more you experience it, the more alive you feel. When you stop growing you feel dead.

Let's start with your body, for sometimes it may seem to you that it is changing almost by the week. Some of you may feel that one night you have gone to bed a boy or a girl and have awakened a man or a woman. Of course, it isn't as sudden as all that, but because we are such creatures of habit, *any* change has to be very gradual indeed if we are not to be surprised by it—and certainly the changes going on between ten and sixteen are not gradual. Yet there is plenty of time for you to get used to them and to understand them.

Sometimes you will notice changes first in your personality—but mostly body and personality go together. And sometimes you won't notice any change in yourself for ever so long, while all your friends seem to be sprouting evidences of manhood and womanhood. This is normal.

Each of us has an inborn predetermined rate of growth—yet by twenty-one we all end up being physically full-grown men or women just the same.

Growth and Changes in Girls

If you are a girl, one of the first physical things you may notice is that your breasts are filling out. Not long after—maybe the very next year—you will notice that your pubic hair (the hair growing over your lower pelvis) has begun to get coarser and curlier.

Within three months you'll probably begin to menstruate. Menstruation is a fascinating process. Most girls consider it something of a nuisance though they may be pleased that now they are officially among the "initiate."

What menstruation means is that your ovaries are beginning to mature and to release egg cells which were already determined at the time of your birth.

It may be a year or two yet before the ovaries will deliver a fully mature ovum (egg) which could be fertilized and grow to be a baby, but the process has begun and theoretically at least you are now capable of conceiving a child if your ovum comes in contact with a sperm cell from a male.

The word *menstruation* comes from the word *menses*, meaning monthly. Beginning in puberty, ovulation occurs once each month. Ovulation means that the ovary of the woman produces an ovum or egg which passes down through the Fallopian tube to the uterus. The uterus prepares a thick lining, rich in blood cells, to nourish the possible guest (the fertilized egg) which will implant itself in this lining. However, if the egg is not fertilized (that is, if no sperm from a male is present in the Fallopian tube as it makes its passage down to the uterus), the egg is simply absorbed into the system. About ten days or so later, the lining sloughs off and passes out of the body as menstrual blood.

Some girls worry when they see the extent of their flow, wondering if they can lose that much blood and not be weakened in some way. I have even known of girls who feared they might bleed to death.

There is no need for such concern. The actual amount of blood is very little—but when mixed with mucus and other secretions, it appears as "all blood." If you try the experiment of dropping a teaspoon of blood in a glass of water, you will see what I mean. Some nutritionists concerned with feminine health have recommended the addition of iron, calcium, and vitamins before and during menstruation. This is something you might like to check out further with your school nurse.

Usually the "flow"—or menstruation period—lasts from three to five days.

Some girls feel a bit droopy a few days before menstruation begins, and a few girls experience varying degrees of discomfort the first day of the flow. Home remedies will usually suffice to make most girls quite comfortable, such as keeping reasonably warm and avoiding strenuous exercise. Also, scientific research has revealed that masturbation to orgasm right at the beginning of menstruation seems to dissolve tension and relieve pain. (If you don't know the meaning of the words *masturbation* or *orgasm*, see pages 32 and 21 of this book.)

If you suffer real pain you should ask to see a good gynecologist who may give you medication for its relief. There is no reason why you should put up with pain in menstruation.

There are some girls who find that their whole nature seems to change during the week or so before they menstruate. This can be quite baffling both to the girl and to her friends—especially to her boy friend, if she has one.

Often he wonders what in the world he did to warrant an irritable response from her, or why it is that she is affectionate one day, and two days later doesn't want to be touched.

Usually such a shift in mood occurs during the progesterone phase of the menstrual cycle, that is, between the time of ovulation and the time bleeding begins. Gynecologists can prescribe hormones to take orally that will modify discomforting mood swings. If you find that you just can't live with yourself in the week before menstruation, by all means get your parents to take you to a gynecologist who has made it his or her business to be sensitive to such matters. He or she will doubtless be able to help you. Steer clear of any outdated doctor who tries to foist moral values on you, such as, "Pain is your lot, oh woman," or "All this will pass once you are married."

Many girls want to know how to take care of themselves during menstruation. The question of personal hygiene is simple. The keynote is cleanliness. You take baths frequently, and make certain that secretions are carefully washed away daily—or oftener if need be. You wear either a sanitary napkin or a tampon to absorb the discharge, and you change these several times daily. When you are through with one, you wrap it in toilet paper carefully so that it won't easily become unwrapped, and deposit it in a wastebasket in the bathroom. You don't flush it down the toilet because it would stop up the plumbing. Neither do you throw it unwrapped in a receptacle because it is often offensive to other people.

You may prefer tampons to sanitary napkins because they are unnoticeable and because napkins tend to chafe the tender area between the legs, which of course tampons do not. It is very easy to insert tampons if you carefully read the instructions on the package. It is a good idea to learn how to use tampons because this is one way that you will get acquainted with your own sexual organs, if you haven't done so before.

If you have just started menstruating, you may prefer sanitary napkins at first; indeed, you may prefer them all your life, feeling that they are, for one reason or another, more comfortable. It is entirely a matter of individual choice.

You may observe that your breasts swell a bit and are sensitive to touch just before menstruation. Here again hormones are at work, stimulating the breast for its future work in producing milk for suckling a baby.

There are changes other than the physical ones that you may notice about yourself. You may find, for example, that you have an increased interest in romancing. You may even find yourself daydreaming about the Prince Charming you hope will come your way. You fantasize that he will literally sweep you off your feet. You may begin to look at every boy as someone more than a companion or play-fellow. You wonder what kind of lover, husband, or father he will make.

Questions such as, "Will he like me?" "How do I look to him?" "Will he notice me?" preoccupy you.

A lot of girls get giggly. Giggliness is really a form of nervousness, and who wouldn't be a little nervous when first moving into unfamiliar territory? But the giggliness passes as you find your way around.

Some girls are sure that they are ugly ducklings and will be among the rejected. Fear of rejection is one of the commonest fears of everyone—even adults. Such irra-tional fear reaches back to so early a time in our lives that we can't rightly remember its beginnings. Its likely origin may be the countless occasions we were left in our cribs to "cry it out" when what we really needed was to be picked up and cuddled. In those days we were desolate—even desperate—in our helplessness. The degree of such infantile anguish was such that most of us carry over into adult life the same fear of *any* rejection. We fail to recognize that as teenagers, for example, and especially as adults, we have many resources we didn't have as infants, such as finding another friend if we are rejected by one.

Rejection is as common a part of everyday life as acceptance. All adults, and I mean *all*, have to learn that rejection is not something dreadful which puts them beyond the pale, but just a normal everyday occurrence, usually reflecting individual differences.

So if you have been rejected here or there, don't assume it is because you are an impossible person, or that you are forever going to be unattractive to all members of the human race, especially the opposite sex.

The funny thing is, you don't have to be beautiful to be attractive. The secret of having people love you is learning how to express your love to them—learning how to pay positive attention to them. We'll talk more about that later, but I want to comfort some of you right now, those who have already and incorrectly come to the conclusion that adolescence is a pretty sticky time of it and that you are doomed to be a wallflower. No girl—and I mean *no* girl—need be one.

Let's go back to those wonderful changes going on in you. There are some that will compel you to intensify your habits of hygiene.

Since your skin glands will be secreting more, you may notice that your pores tend to get clogged up and that you break out in acne (pimples). Also, your hair may get oilier than usual. This simply means that you'll have to bathe and shampoo oftener. A mild soap and water will usually do the trick. The additional attention you'll have to give such matters now may be a nuisance—but it is worth it. By the time you're eighteen or so, your glands will settle down and the habits of fastidiousness you have established will add to your charm as a woman. You may notice changes in your voice too; gradually, it becomes richer and fuller and more womanly.

One of the really baffling things to get used to is understanding what is expected of you by the outside world. At one moment, because you've suddenly grown so big physically, you're expected to behave like a grown-up. The next moment, you're treated as if you were still back in kindergarten.

It helps to ask the adults who control your life what they really do expect of you, and it helps them for you to say what you really think can be expected of you.

These are the years when conformity in external matters, like dress, seems to be very important. I can well remember a period when each of my teenage daughters felt she had to telephone some other girl to find out what was being worn that day at school before choosing her own attire. This didn't last very long, but you may find yourself going through it, just the same, even if you had been quite independent before.

Sometimes you may be tempted to daydream more than to study. This is natural. On the other hand, these are also the years when you will have to study hard if you are to fulfill your own potential.

Growth and Changes in Boys

Thus far I've talked about changes that go on in girls in the early teens. What about boys? Those that occur for boys are equally exciting, sometimes bewildering, and actually not too different.

Some time between ten and fifteen, if you are a boy, you begin to grow hair on your chest, your back, your arms, your face, and especially on the pubic area just above your penis. This hair at first will be soft and downy, but it will gradually darken and become coarser.

Just as a girl rejoices in her budding breasts, many of you boys will take delight when the first soft fuzz begins to appear on your face.

About this time you will also experience a voice change. You may feel for a while that your voice is out of control—as if you have laryngitis, but eventually it will stabilize and you will have a deeper, fuller, mature man's voice.

This is the time of puberty. Puberty means that sperm cells are beginning to be manufactured in your testicles (oval shaped glands lying within your scrotum) and you become able to ejaculate (send out) a liquid (called seminal fluid) when you experience orgasm (climax of sexual pleasure—usually accompanied by the ejaculation of semen). Often the first knowledge you have of the presence of seminal fluid is when you have what is called a *wet dream*. The technical term for *wet dream* is *nocturnal emission*.

This simply means that sufficient sperm cells combined with seminal fluid have been stored in the seminal vesicles so that release is desirable. Mother Nature takes care of this for a boy by expelling the accumulated liquid through an ejaculation which occurs in sleep.

You may wonder what in blazes your mother will say when she sees this sticky substance on your pajamas. But you can be reassured by the knowledge that normal, healthy mothers welcome such a sight as evidence that their sons are maturing normally, just as they welcome menstruation in their daughters as a similar landmark of normal development.

Mothers may seem to want to keep you in rompers for life, but this is really not the case. On the whole, parents are far more worried if you don't mature than if you do.

Incidentally, the usual age range for such maturation can be anywhere from ten to fifteen. I've never quite determined in my own mind which is easier for a boy or girl, maturing way ahead of friends, or way behind them. I've heard bitter complaints at both ends of the scale. I suppose if you could have your "druthers," you'd be lucky to be right in the middle. However, you might as well learn to be philosophical about this matter, for there is not one thing you can do about it. Your growth pattern is hereditary, and in due time, no matter how many boys are ahead of you or behind you, you'll even out, reaching your full development at about age twenty or twenty-one.

Boys as well as girls do a lot of daydreaming in adolescence. Some of you may write poetry for the first time in your lives (it's too bad you don't go on writing it later—for this side of you could make all of your life more rich and colorful). One trouble with adult males is that there has been such a taboo against expressing the romantic, the poetic, and the tender that your own very wonderful urge is too often snuffed out. Women wish it wouldn't be.

Boys are quite a bit different from girls in one respect, however. While girls may romanticize about boys, boys are more likely to have quite specifically sexual feelings about girls. Boys are enormously aroused sexually by coquettishness in girls, by visual displays of female beauty, and by physical closeness. All this may change, of course, as girls get more in touch with their own good sexual feelings and are allowed to express them.

A boy can be quite startled at how fast his penis becomes hard and erect at the very sight of a sexy girl— sometimes by just the thought of her.

At first some boys are embarrassed, feeling that all the world can see what's happening down there in their pants. But rarely is this so, for people just don't make a habit of staring at that part of the anatomy. They are much more likely to be paying attention to faces if they are paying attention at all.

So getting used to frequent erections under all sorts of erotic stimulants is one of the things you as a boy have to learn.

After a while you will discover that these erections can give you a pleasurable sense of well-being and aliveness, and that you don't really *have* to ejaculate every time your penis feels excited. In fact, learning how to enjoy and prolong such pleasure is an art worth acquiring.

A great many boys have been misinformed by older boys or men that their masculinity depends on having intercourse with whomever and however it can be accomplished. This is far from true.

Good masculine feelings come from learning how to handle sexual urges so that you can enjoy them without jeopardizing yourself or anyone else, and without disassociating your sexual expressions from your love feelings.

Boys in puberty, like girls, tend to develop a gang instinct. You may find, for a while at least, that being one of the gang is more important than following through your own individual hobbies. You may feel that it is more imperative that you make the football team than that you fulfill yourself in your earlier favorite pastimes.

A boy in puberty is experiencing the action of the male hormones in his system. For a time he, like the girl, may have a problem with skin unless he is meticulously careful to use soap and water generously, and even then he may not completely escape some evidence of acne (pimples).

There was a time when boys were frightened by misinformed teachers who told them their skin would break out in pimples if they masturbated. Of course this isn't true. The reverse would be closer to the truth because the comfortable discharge of excessive tension through relaxed masturbation would tend to minimize rather than maximize skin problems. We will talk more about masturbation later, and the many myths related to it.

As a boy of twelve to fifteen, your sexual urge may be many times greater than that of most girls of your own age. This can add up to a discrepancy in goals between you, and may account for a lot of the apparent disharmony between you and your girl friend.

In Chapter 4, "Safe Sex," I plan to tell you of some of the creative ways you can solve this problem, but for now let's try to understand your body better because, after all, it is through your body that you will express your sexuality.

2 Anatomy

Your Sexual Body and What Makes You Male or Female

The Boy's Sex Organs

If you are a boy, your external sex organs are your penis and your scrotum. Within the scrotum lie your testicles, which are the male sex glands. They have two extremely important functions: first, to secrete male sex hormones into the blood, and second, to produce sperm, which are the seeds of future life. These, when united with the female egg under the proper circumstances, will result in the birth of a baby.

The scrotum also contains a complicated system of ducts and vesicles through which the sperm are conducted and stored.

The penis has a loose flap of skin (called the foreskin, or the prepuce) over the tip (called the glans). (Circumcision is the surgical removal of this foreskin, usually done shortly after birth.) The urethra, a tube or opening seen in the glans, serves as a passage for liquid wastes from the bladder. The same tube also serves for the passage of seminal fluid containing sperm.

After sperm are manufactured by the testicles, they are then passed into a series of tiny tubicles, called the epididimus (also located in the scrotum), where they are matured and sent along through a duct to the seminal vesicles. The seminal vesicles manufacture a fluid that mixes with the sperm—and the resulting substance is called semen, or seminal fluid. This fluid is stored in the seminal vesicles until it becomes desirable to release it, and then it discharges, either through a "wet dream" or through direct stimulation of the penis (as in masturbation or in intercourse), or it can simply be absorbed into the bloodstream with no harm to the system and no discharge taking place.

The mechanism of discharge, or release of seminal fluid, is called ejaculation.

Ejaculation is usually experienced as highly pleasurable and when this deep pleasure is felt it is called orgasm. A boy generally—but not necessarily—has an orgasm when he has an ejaculation.

Of course, many times in your life before puberty when you experienced orgasm, you did so *without* ejaculation; but from puberty onward orgasm is fairly regularly accompanied by ejaculation—in other words, by the presence of seminal fluid.

You usually ejaculate about a teaspoon of a smooth milky substance which contains literally millions of spermatozoa (seed). It takes only one of these seeds uniting with an ovum in a female body to start the development of a baby.

Many boys and girls wonder how the very same duct in the penis can be utilized for both the passage of urine and the passage of seminal fluid without one contaminating the other or there being a need for two tubes.

Here is where one of the miracles of nature makes itself especially apparent. Opposing sets of muscles go into operation to control the flow of urine or the release of seminal fluid; one set contracts, blocking off the flow of urine, the other relaxes and releases the ejaculate from its storehouse in the seminal vesicles. The triggering mechanism for ejaculation is in itself quite fascinating.

First, of course, the penis must become erect. Erection of the penis occurs when the hollow bodies in the penis become suddenly filled with blood and the penis thus becomes comparatively rigid. Erection itself can be caused by many stimuli: through the mind by exciting sexual thoughts, through direct touch and caressing of the penis, by friction of clothing, by the pressure of a full bladder or full seminal vesicles, or from sex hormones in the bloodstream.

When any one, or any combination of several stimuli, reaches a certain degree of intensity, the ejaculatory mechanism is triggered and ejaculation occurs.

The Girl's Sex Organs

Let's turn to you, the girl, for a moment and compare your sexual anatomy with the boy's.

Instead of testicles you have ovaries. These are located in your abdomen, one on each side. It is here that the eggs, or ova, are manufactured. Once each month, under the triggering stimulation of hormones, a fully ripe egg (ovum) is secreted. It leaves its egg "factory" (ovary) through a passage called the Fallopian tube and descends into the uterus (or womb). The uterus is an incredible organ in itself. Pearlike in shape and a bit smaller in size, it can expand to hold a fully matured baby weighing anywhere from six to nine pounds. (There are babies born as large as twelve pounds. Or imagine triplets living in that amazing womb.)

Descending from the uterus is a passage called the cervical canal, which empties into the vagina. The vagina is a pocketlike opening into which the penis fits when a male mates with a female, and it is into this pocket that he ejaculates, depositing his seminal fluid containing sperm.

Like the boy, you have external sex organs. Your clitoris, located in approximately the same position on your body as the boy's penis on his body, is really like a tiny penis, though it has only a single function, not a dual one like the boy's. The word clitoris comes from the Greek word meaning key—and the clitoris is well named, for it is indeed the key to your sexual pleasure.

Just as the penis is enormously pleasurably sensitive, so is the clitoris, including the area surrounding it which is rich in nerve endings that, when stimulated by caressing touch, send messages of pleasure back to the brain.

Surrounding the clitoris and the vaginal opening are large outer lips (labia majora), and within those is a smaller set of lips (labia minora).

Just below the clitoris but above the vagina is the urethra, which is the opening through which a girl urinates. Unlike a boy, you have completely separate passages for the expulsion of your urinary and sexual secretions. (Though some girls grow up thinking they urinate through their clitoris, just as a boy urinates through his penis, this is not true.)

Your vagina is a remarkable organ in itself, capable of supplying you with additional pleasure, and is expandable to receive your own finger, a tampon, or a penis, and even to serve as the passage through which a baby may be born.

Your anus, through which bowel movements are excreted, is located in the same place on your body as is the boy's.

Just within the entrance to your vagina are two tiny glands called the Bartholin glands. These secrete lubricating fluids at the moment of orgasm. There are also sweat glands that secrete lubrication during sexual excitation.

What Is a Virgin?

In girls who have never had sexual intercourse, a tissue called a *hymen* partially covers the opening to the vagina.

Of course, there is always an opening through this through which the menstrual blood and other secretions can be expelled, so an intact hymen is not a kind of birth control, as some people think. Some girls are born without hymens. Also, the hymens of many girls are ruptured through physical activities, like riding a horse, strenuous exercise, or sports. On the other hand, the hymens of other girls are so thick and resistive that it is necessary for them to have a slight surgical operation (under local anesthetic) before the vagina can be penetrated.

The presence or absence of a hymen does not determine whether you are a virgin or not. The word *virgin* means one (male or female) who has never had sexual intercourse.

There was a time when women were considered the property or the chattel of men. Since the control of birth was not understood, and since the children inherited the possessions of the father, a very strict custom grew up among men demanding that a girl who was to be a wife must be a virgin at the time a man accepted her in marriage.

Since the presence or absence of a hymen was often the determining factor in establishing virginity, can you imagine the heartache and injustice that was often done women whose hymens were broken but who were in fact virgins? Some very funny, very sad tales are told of women who spread red ink or an animal's blood on the sheet after their marriage night just to prove to an adamant husband that he had properly broken the hymen himself.

Actually, a hymen is of no use whatsoever, and the modern male feels about it just the way he might about his girl friend having an appendix. It doesn't matter.

In a very young girl, the presence of a hymen might deter her and an aggressive boy friend from too early sexual intercourse, which fact might serve her in good stead.

But when a girl is grown, a hymen is just a nuisance which will sooner or later have to be obliterated, and certainly it is not an evidence of virginity.

Breasts are an important part of your sexual anatomy. While boys have rudimentary breasts, they do not have the kind of sex hormones that will trigger their development. Your female hormones, on the other hand, prepare your breasts for the suckling of babies. In addition to their function of providing nourishment to your future babies, your breasts also have a great many sensitive nerve endings which, when stimulated, bring you sensuous pleasure. Most people consider breasts very beautiful.

Erogenous Zones

Let us discuss the role of the nerves in sexual excitation and pleasure.

In both men and women we speak of "erogenous zones." This simply means those areas of the body that contain unusual numbers of nerve endings which when stimulated conduct messages to the brain which we interpret not only as pleasurable, but as sexually exciting. That is, their excitation makes us feel "sexy" —makes us specifically want to engage in sexual intercourse or other genital activity such as masturbation, or mutual caressing of the genital organs.

These erogenous zones are the ears and earlobes, lips, under the arms, the area around the nipples (and, in women, the whole breast area), the skin over the pelvis, the buttocks, the lower spine, the anus, the penis and the testicles (in men), the clitoris and labia and vaginal opening (in women), and the inner and outer surfaces of the upper thighs.

Later on when we talk about the use of artistry in lovemaking, it will be important for you to recall these areas of erogenous stimulation.

Psychologic stimuli have a great deal to do with sexuality, of course, and we will discuss this later.

Hormones and Sexuality

We have only touched on the role of hormones. Let us discuss them further as they affect you sexually.

The pituitary is the master gland. In the female, it stimulates the ovaries to secrete and to produce a hormone which starts egg production, the process of menstruation, and the changes which take place in pregnancy.

Estrogen is the name of the hormone secreted by the ovaries; estrogen is also called the *female* hormone. In fact, it is the ovary that makes a woman "female." If women have to have their ovaries removed, as some women have had to do when they have suffered cancer of the ovaries, they tend to lose something of their physical femininity, unless they have hormone replacement therapy.

In women approaching menopause (ages forty-five to fifty), when the ovaries stop producing eggs, the pituitary gland may become disturbed and its control over the other glands and the nervous system is temporarily affected. This accounts for the nervous irritability of some women at this time, and also for their hot and cold "flashes." It is most wise for a woman approaching menopause to have her doctor make regular estrogen-level checks. If her system needs estrogen, it can be administered to her orally in the form of pills which aid her enormously in feeling like the normally lovely woman she always was. It does not, of course, change the fact that she will not produce babies after she has completed menopause.

I speak of menopause because so many of your mothers may be experiencing the baffling phenomenon called "change of life," and may not have had the medical help which is available. It may help you to understand some of the curious and seemingly unreasonable swings in mood of your mother. Perhaps you might suggest to her tactfully that an estrogen-level check may be in order.

What about male sex glands? What make a man "male," of course, are his testicles, which produce sperm. He too, however, like the woman, has a pituitary gland (that master gland which triggers the action of all the other glands).

The sex hormone secreted by the male is called androgen. Without this hormone a boy would more resemble a girl than a boy. The presence of male hormones in his bloodstream is responsible for his deep voice, his muscular shoulders, his narrow hips, his hair distribution.

If a man is castrated, that is, if his testicles are removed, he becomes incapable of producing sperm cells and also begins to lose his sex power (potency). If the castration takes place before puberty, he never does develop potency. (His voice remains high; his musculature looks more like a girl's than a boy's.)

In ancient times a very cruel practice of conquering tribes in time of war was to castrate the males of the conquered people. These castrated men were then called eunuchs—and were used as slaves. A man without his testicles is usually a very passive and tractable man indeed.

That is why we say to this day that a man without aggressive male courage "has lost his balls."

We also speak of "psychological castration." This simply means that someone has made a boy so afraid of or ashamed of his maleness that he acts like a man who has been physically castrated.

Some mothers treat their sons that way, and a great many girls unknowingly treat their boy friends so as to reduce their pride in manhood—which is a cruel thing to do. We speak of such women as "psychological castrators."

I wouldn't want to leave this discussion of the

mechanics of sex without saying a word about the brain—which is the master tool of both the mind and the imagination.

All kinds of stimuli—sight, sound, smell, taste, touch —are relayed to the brain which, through associative mechanisms, get linked with sexuality.

For example, the sight of a pretty girl or an emotionally moving film about a strong man's heroism may stir you sexually as much as, or maybe more than, direct touch stimulation. Just thinking about loving or being loved may start the sexual juices flowing.

If you have heard a certain tune or smelled a certain fragrance, or been in a certain environment where you also felt sexually stimulated, then the repetition of that tune, that fragrance, that place can of itself induce sexual feeling.

This is called "conditioned learning." A Russian named Pavlov wrote a great deal about conditioned learning. One of his original experiments was with hungry dogs. Each time he fed these dogs he also rang a bell. After a bit, all he had to do was ring the bell and the dogs started salivating. Salivation is not under conscious control; that is, you can't just salivate by telling yourself to do so, but if you imagine the world's most delicious dinner, you might find yourself dripping from the mouth before you know it.

Sexual feeling thus is often stimulated by mental images.

③ Intercourse

What, When, Where, and How to Do It Without Being a Selfish Pig

Nearly every young person I have ever talked with wants to know how sex works—how do people mate, do they like it? Does it feel good, does it hurt? Do they have intercourse only when they want a baby? Can they make love without getting a baby? And a host of other questions of this sort.

Safety and Mutual Love

In later chapters I'm going to talk about birth control and pregnancy, so for now let's just talk about the art and science of intercourse. There are many slang words for *intercourse*, such as *fuck*, *screw*, *lay*, *ball*, and so on. Their use nearly always depreciates intercourse as an act of love, but sometimes they are used merely for fun or because of ignorance.

Intercourse is when a man inserts his erect penis into the vagina of a woman, and by a series of in-and-out movements stimulates himself—and ideally her too—to the point where he ejaculates semen. This ejaculatory moment for him is what is generally called orgasm. Her body also may reach a peak of pleasurable tension which ultimately "explodes" into a series of convulsivelike movements which at their finish leaves her relaxed and content. This is orgasm for her. She may, in fact, have more than one orgasm, or she may have none, and we'll talk about this later.

The seminal fluid that is discharged through his penis is retained in her body, and millions of infinitesimal sperm begin instantly to swim up her cervical canal into her uterus and from there up her Fallopian tube—in search of an egg to fertilize. If the timing has been right for the girl and an egg is traveling down the tube, she may become pregnant. If no egg is present—no pregnancy.

Generally, for the man, this is all very pleasurable; in fact, one of the most pleasurable kinds of experience that he can know.

It can also be just as pleasurable for the woman if she and the man know a few facts that until recently were known only by relatively few couples.

Here are some of these facts.

Sexual intercourse, if it is to be deeply pleasurable and satisfying to a man and a woman, has to be carried on in an atmosphere of mutual love and trust.

Each partner has to be committed to the other's well-being rather than seeking only his or her own selfish sensuous pleasure. Given such a relationship, they choose to enjoy intercourse under conditions that are safe for both of them.

Such safety can exist in marriage where the partners have shown themselves able to make a home for each other and support themselves, and have given many evidences of mutual love. Such safety may also exist in committed relationships prior to or outside of marriage, but always there are present many evidences of mutual love.

What do such couples need to know in order to have a fulfilling sexual experience? First, each partner must know how to sexually excite and stimulate the other. Each must know how to praise and express appreciation of the other so that each feels utterly happy and relaxed in the other's presence. Each must put aside false modesty and allow himself or herself to see the beauty in the other's body, including the genital organs.

How many of you girls, for example, have ever been encouraged to look with awe and wonder at the erect penis of a male—even a statue of a male—or a work of art portraying one?

Boys have the advantage over girls here, for girls' bodies are portrayed everywhere for men to appreciate and enjoy visually. Girls seldom have this same chance to see a boy's body, though this is changing.

There was a time in history, you know, when male figures were shown in all their glory, and even further back in time there was phallic worship (worship of the penis). I am told that the earliest churches were built in the shape of a phallus (penis) and that, try as they would, the Jewish and later the Christian architects could not persuade the more primitive peoples to give up their penis-shaped places of worship; so the architects compromised by putting pointed steeples on top of the penis-shaped towers, and this is the origin of steeples. This story may or may not be true, but perhaps it may serve to get you thinking about the penis as something beautiful and deserving of wonder.

Many girls have been taught that their own genital organs are not beautiful either. What a pity. Actually, they are exquisite. The labia (lips surrounding the vagina) are like opening petals of an extraordinarily lovely flower which reveals a tiny bud (the clitoris) above and the silken promise of warm womblike comfort below.

Both the penis and the vagina are so delicately lovely to touch and their fragrance is so sweet that the poets of the ages have gone out of their way to write about them.

If you like, read The Song of Solomon in the Bible in which Solomon and his beloved express to each other their aesthetic reaction to each other's bodies. These may surprise you.

Naturally, both men and women must be fastidiously clean about their genital organs if these are to be perceived as I have described them. Every girl needs to learn while she is yet very young how to push back the foreskin that covers her clitoris and wash daily, just as an uncircumcised boy needs to push back his foreskin and wash. Even one who *has* been circumcised must learn to wash his whole genital area thoroughly before making love.

Next, if a man and a woman are to experience pleasure in intercourse, both must be aware of the most important erogenous zones of the other: the earlobes, lips, breasts, abdomen, pelvis, buttocks, genitals.

The man most particularly must remember that the area around the clitoris of the woman must be stimulated, both before and during intercourse, if she is to enjoy intercourse as much as he does. By stimulation I don't mean friction right on the tip of the sensitive little bud of a clitoris, but all around it, mobilizing it, playing with it, making sure that it is well lubricated. The genital "skin" secretes a liquid under sexual excitation, and this acts as lubrication. However, if a woman or man is a bit anxious, these juices are not secreted in enough quantity nor fast enough to be effective. Therefore, the need to use additional lubricants, such as cold cream, KY jelly, or, most practically, saliva from the man's or woman's own mouth.

Such pleasurable excitation prepares the woman to receive the penis just as hungrily, as eagerly, as the man is to give it to her.

At this point he slides it into her vagina, often guided by her hand. Both partners then move their pelvises in and out, back and forth, up and down, in a series of rhythmical movements not unlike a dance. A great philosopher, Havelock Ellis, called it "the dance of life."

If they have been skillful, if they have been emotionally moved by each other's love, both will reach a peak of pleasurable intensity so great that in each it bursts as an explosive series of quivering contractions that literally shake their whole bodies. At this moment the man ejaculates and the woman's vagina expands and contracts again and again for several moments in an ecstasy of pleasure. In the moments just before their orgasm, their hearts beat faster. Their breath is accelerated; sometimes one or both let out a little cry or groan, tears, or even a shout of pleasure, and then—after the climax or orgasm—both lie still, relaxing in each other's arms, content, warm, renewed. This whole act may have taken only two or three minutes—or it may have taken an hour or more, depending on the individuals. The average man takes less than two minutes to come to orgasm. The average woman is said to take thirty minutes. This is why it is wise for a man to train himself to extend his pleasure for as long as possible so as to give the woman a chance to "come" in her own time.

"Coming" together is a peak experience; however, like most peak experiences, it does not happen with regularity. What can and should happen, however, is that each partner should arrive at orgasmic release and pleasure before any given lovemaking episode is completed. Thus, despite some old myths, coming together is not necessary for total enjoyment of both.

There are many positions in which human beings can accomplish the act of intercourse. In fact, any position at all in which it is possible for the penis to be inserted in the vagina is included in the many varieties of ways that men and women have managed it. The most usual position in our culture is for the woman to lie on her back, her knees slightly bend and spread apart. The man lies on top of her, face-to-face, supporting his weight on his elbows. This is jokingly called the missionary position because it is said that the pope decreed that man should dominate woman, and also it was known by then that women became pregnant more easily in this position. However, it may please a given couple more to have the man lie on his back and the woman lie on top of him.

Many boys and girls, having watched dogs copulate, have wondered if this is the way humans do it too. Some do, but most do not.

The position chosen by any given couple is a highly individual matter, mostly determined by their preferences. Sometimes, however, it is determined by the way they are built or on their desire to achieve pregnancy by their union.

For example, if a woman has a tipped uterus, it may not be sufficiently mobile when an object like a penis pushes against the cervix, and this may cause her pain. Therefore, the man must try a different position for intercourse, one that permits his penis to slide down at an angle so as not to collide with her cervix.

When a man and a woman go to the doctor for an examination before having intercourse, the doctor can advise the woman right away whether or not her womb is tipped, and the man, acting on the information, can from the very first use positions for intercourse that will not give her pain.

Often the position used for intercourse depends more on how much the woman needs continuous clitoral stimulation from the man than on any other factor. Many, if not most, women depend on such stimulation right to the moment of orgasm. They can rarely achieve enough contact of the woman's clitoris with the man's penis unless they (a) are in a position so that the man can easily free one of his hands to fondle her clitoris while keeping his penis inside her, or (b) both learn how to "rock and roll"—that is, swing their pelvises rhythmically toward and away from each other for a long enough time so that friction of the clitoris occurs. The success of the latter method, of course, depends on a man's being able to remain in disciplined control of the timing of his ejaculation.

Young men often wonder if the size of their penis will affect the way a young woman enjoys intercourse. Actually not. The skill of use is the important thing—and, as I mentioned earlier, the ability to stimulate her clitoral area. A big penis doesn't mean virility any more than big breasts mean femininity.

Many young men and women wonder if first intercourse will hurt—will breaking the hymen (that tiny perforated membrane covering the entrance to the vagina) bother the female? It need not. You, as a thoughtful young man, can take time, often over a number of petting experiences, to slowly insert one well-lubricated finger into her vagina. When she has gotten used to that, you can insert two and gently stretch the opening. This gradual preparation for the reception of your penis will avoid for her any pain or discomfort whatsoever—and will also dissipate fear of intercourse, which some young women do have.

If you are a young woman you can take responsibility for opening yourself also. Sometimes a gynecologist will give you hymen stretchers to stretch your own opening. These are simply a series of graduated tubes, usually made of rubber or plastic and rounded at the end, with which you can practice insertion until you are stretched to the point where the largest one does not feel uncomfortable. You are instructed to lubricate them well and gently press, moving them in and out. Doing this in a warm bathtub may help relax muscular tension. Your own fingers, or those of your lover, may be the best of all hymen-stretchers.

You may have a very thick and resistive hymen and, if so, you should have it surgically removed under anesthesia by a physician. This should be done at least six weeks before intercourse is attempted so that the area will have time to heal comfortably.

When Can I Have Intercourse?

Some boys and girls wonder what are the preliminaries to mating. "How do you ask a woman to have intercourse with you?" is a common question, and, "When do you do it?"

In marriage people can have intercourse more or less whenever they feel like it. Some partners want to enjoy each other's bodies every night. Others feel like intercourse once or twice a week, and occasionally there are couples who want it once a month or so. Thus sexual desire is highly variable, depending on many factors. The average for most young couples is about three times a week.

People make love not just to create babies, as I have already explained, but to be renewed and comforted by closeness and for the sheer joyous pleasure they have in the act.

Partners who communicate well with each other about sex are easily able to express their desires. Each tends to gravitate to the other with unmistakable invitations. In premarital lovemaking generally, a boy and girl have many petting experiences that have initiated them to the sexual needs and desires of each other. If they are wise, and if they care for each other, they have also talked over and have prepared for the act of intercourse so that there is no need to "ask for" intercourse on an impulse basis.

When two people love each other, trust each other completely, and know each other well, embarrassment and fear of sexual intercourse tend to vanish. The girl who thought she would be afraid of intercourse discovers in the relaxation resulting from the atmosphere of trust that she is no longer afraid.

Occasionally, however, young men or women will carry right into adulthood a terrifying fear of sexuality. This is always because he or she was badly conditioned in childhood or has suffered some frightening experience. It would be well for such a person to see a therapist before marriage or before entering a committed relationship with another person. Most sexual fears and inadequacies can be dissipated with sensitive professional help.

In very few other life experiences does the character structure of two individuals emerge as clearly as it does as they approach sexual intercourse. Irresponsibility, selfishness, and inconsiderateness are instantly apparent. If sexual intercourse is to be experienced as the recreative blessing it can be, it requires the utmost of generosity, trustworthiness, and tested love from both participants.

Many young teenagers, when thinking about sexual intercourse, imagine that they can achieve these joys simply by trying out intercourse with the first person who says "I love you, I need you, I want you." If they make the mistake of attempting it on such a flimsy basis, the result will be very much like that of two children who have built a playhouse out of a blanket and two chairs. It looks easy at first, but it collapses with the first breath of wind or removal of a chair.

I need not tell you that a durable house must be built of durable materials by skilled and devoted persons if it is not to fall apart. Sexual intercourse is like that, too. It requires two loving partners, each of whom cares as much for the well-being of the other as for his or her own, having demonstrated that love in many ways.

Sexual intercourse thus, if it is to be mutually rewarding, involves a great deal more than sex games (house play) or temporarily pleasurable fantasies.

Can you imagine yourself as a fifteen-year-old being able to care in a fully responsible way for the well-being of a partner? You would have to be a Superman or a Wonder Woman to have undergone the necessary discipline to have become economically independent and capable of having entrusted to you another person's future health. Of course, you might manage this if you had the full support and backing of parents.

Yet many young people take on sexual intercourse prematurely. They may fall for verbal expressions of love which really mask only sexual urges crying out for release. A young man is able to have intercourse as soon as he can maintain an erection, but it is only really satisfying when he has met many other conditions. For a girl, even if she doesn't get pregnant, intercourse without emotional safeguards leaves the experience less than satisfying.

Any young man worth his salt wants his partner to experience the same joy he experiences. If time after time she doesn't, he begins to think about himself as a selfish pig. His self-esteem goes down. There is hardly anything worse for us than the lowering of our self-esteem.

Here are what I think are the minimum requirements for both partners for successful and rewarding sexual intercourse:

1. Maturation of body, male and female (somewhere between seventeen and twenty-one).

2. Thorough training in the use of birth control.

3. Full willingness and preparedness to care for a baby, or to have an abortion, should there be an accident in the use of birth control.

4. Emotional commitment of one to the other whether or not marriage is intended.

5. Ability to acquire skills that will bring sexual satisfaction to both partners.

6. Economic independence, if needed, or agreement of parents to provide support.

7. A protected environment.

8. A conscience that is free of guilt, knowing that it has complied with all those conditions necessary for safe and

satisfying sexual intercourse, and is not burdened with religious or other taboos.

Rare is the boy or girl under seventeen who can meet these conditions.

I am sure you will wonder how the tribal customs of whole population groups have survived child marriages. Please remember that they may have survived (with adult supervision and protection), but they have not prevailed.

4 Safe Sex

Can I Enjoy the Water Without Getting in Over My Head?

Autoeroticism: Self-Pleasuring

After reading the last chapter, you may have the impression that the enjoyment of sex has to be limited to adults who are married or in committed relationships. It does not.

At your age, you have several ways to experience sexuality which can be as pleasurable as intercourse is to adults. Furthermore, these ways do not plunge you into tragedies, nor do they demand adult responsibilities, which force you to grow beyond your years.

I am talking specifically of self-pleasuring and mutual petting to orgasm.

Unfortunately, the good act of bringing yourself sexual pleasure is attached to a word that has unpleasant connotations—*masturbation*. It stems from two Latin words meaning "to pollute with the hand." No one but a nasty-minded adult, influenced by the perverted mores of his time, could have given such a disgusting name to so pleasantly satisfying an act. Young children use a phrase which is more appropriate. They say, "I'm playing with myself." But there are two scientifically correct terms that also describe the act of caressing one's own genital organs. They are *autoeroticism* and *self-gratification*. Both have a much nicer sound than *masturbation*, and set up more positive images in your mind.

Autoeroticism begins in earliest childhood if it has not been forbidden by some frightened and misinformed adult who was conditioned to think that it might have bad consequences. It continues throughout life (a fact that may surprise you).

It is particularly useful to you during early adolescence as a release for sexual tension. But it is more than that. Through autoeroticism you can become pleasantly at home with your own sexual organs. Also, if it is true that "the moments that make us happy make us wise," then your sheer delight of sensation as you make contact with your developing genitalia will tend to make you wiser about your own sexuality. You will learn the pathway to orgasm and establish your ability to come to climax so that you need never fear for lack of that capacity later on in life. This is not a problem for most men—but because of cultural taboos about sexuality, it can be an enormous problem for many women. Just imagine for a moment how Chinese women with their bound feet had to learn to walk after the bindings were removed in a free adult life. Many of our own women of today are like those Chinese women—in the sex department. When the bindings (inhibitions) are removed, their sexuality just doesn't function. It is, in a sense, atrophied as any other part of the body atrophies with disuse, and it can be a tough therapeutic task to teach such women to use their sexual equipment satisfyingly with a partner.

But girls who learn to bring themselves to orgasm need never have that kind of problem.

Each boy and girl who practices autoeroticism develops a distinctive pattern, unique to himself or herself. Some boys, for example, lie on their stomach and bring friction on their penis by moving their hips up and down against the bed, much as men do in intercourse later on. The majority of boys hold their penis in their hand and bring friction by some sort of caressing manipulation—each boy's movement being quite individualized to his own needs.

Girls' autoerotic patterns are varied also. Some stroke the area around the clitoris in a circular movement, others find that stretching and then releasing the clitoris is more pleasurable; others slip a smooth elliptical object in and out of their vagina with one hand while playing with their clitoris with the other; some squeeze, then relax, their inner thighs, while contracting and relaxing the muscles of the vagina—and so on. The variations are many. A girl may discover very quickly that she needs a lubricating substance if genital friction is to be pleasurable. She may be delighted to find that her own organs secrete a smooth slippery substance that serves her needs, or she may apply cold cream or KY jelly—or saliva from her own mouth.

You will notice that fantasies of all sorts arise from autoeroticism. These tend to excite you sexually. They can also enrich the experience proportional to your ability to use your imagination.

Girls' characteristic fantasies tend to be quite different from those of boys. Generally a girl is more excited by romantic dreams of a lover sweeping her off her feet and carrying her to some beauteous bower where she is made love to exquisitely.

A boy may fantasize a vision of a female nude. Some boys use a picture of a pinup girl to stimulate their erotic feelings. Girls, on the other hand, seem to desire emotional content in their autoerotic dreams.

Fantasies are as varied as people, however, and each person discovers for him- or herself what is pleasurable.

If your fantasy is bizarre, really wild I mean, don't let it worry you. It doesn't mean that you are a pervert in any sense of the word. Many people have bizarre fantasies—there is a certain excitement, after all, in the taboo—but people rarely act on them. You may imagine yourself in a harem, for example, but this doesn't mean that you are in any danger of entering one.

There is one cautionary comment that I would make to boys in particular. Learn, right from the beginning, to extend your autoerotic experience as long in time as you can. Let it be slow and leisurely. The reason: later on you will discover that your female partner will probably be much slower in achieving a level of excitation that can result in orgasm for her. It is desirable for man and woman to synchronize their lovemaking to some degree if they wish to arrive at orgasm together. You can thus see how it would help you later to have conditioned yourself in your teen years to a leisurely way of coming to orgasm. Just so that you can see the logic of this, you should know that a great many women take thirty minutes or more to come to orgasm, while most men take only two or three. One way to handle this discrepancy is for the man to caress the woman's clitoral area with his hands or with his tongue for as long as it takes to bring her to orgasm.

Unfortunately, many boys are so afraid of getting caught masturbating that they train themselves to "come quickly"—most often in the bathroom and before their suspicious mothers can say, "What are you doing in there so long, Henry?"

I hope that in the near future we can *educate mothers and fathers* to relax and be glad about your autoeroticism. In the meantime you might find a safe and protected place like your bedroom, with the door locked, where you can enjoy self-gratification in privacy, safety, and with leisure.

I would also caution both boys and girls not to let the ease of autoeroticism deter you from the more difficult, more highly evolved task of developing social relationships. Occasionally, a boy or girl feels so inadequate socially that he or she retreats inside himself or herself and falls back on self-gratification as a baby might fall back on thumb-sucking. There is absolutely nothing wrong with either sucking a thumb or with autoeroticism as an active and positive sexual experience. Quite the contrary; but these pleasures should not be used as substitutes for further social development which could lead you into future sexual activity with another person.

Myths About Masturbation

Boys and girls hear all sorts of intimations of the dire consequences of masturbation. They are false. There are no dire consequences except the consequence of feeling unnecessarily guilty. We all suffer if we feel guilty. Perhaps when you understand what a positive act autoeroticism is—how it contributes to your sexual development rather than the reverse—you will dissolve whatever guilty feelings you have acquired. I hope so.

One very common misstatement found in some books on sex and morals is this one: "Masturbation is all right if you don't do it too much."

Such a statement sets up a lot of anxiety because every intelligent person then begins to wonder "How much is too much?" The correct answer is that autoeroticism is self-limiting. This means that each person determines his or her own normal frequency by his or her own needs. In a way it is like eating. If you eat too much, you feel uncomfortable. If you masturbate too much, it ceases to be gratifying, at least until you have worked up a hunger for it again.

Furthermore, there are enormous differences between individuals. Some seem to burst with sexual energy that simply shouts for release every day in the week—sometimes several times a day. Others can be happily satisfied by a once-a-month experience. Frequency of need for self-gratification also depends on what else is going on in your life. If you are enormously involved in some engrossing activity that captivates all your attention, the result may be a temporary shoving aside of your sexual urges.

But this is only temporary. By and large, when you are not afraid of your own sexuality, it will emerge in its own good time to the degree that is in harmony with your own nature and your energy.

Perhaps this would be a good time to dissipate the common but erroneous notion that autoeroticism is an "infantile" or "immature" or "antisocial" form of sexuality which adults leave behind when they marry or have sexual partners.

This is simply not true. Autoeroticism is a *different* kind of expression of sexuality from intercourse, but not an immature one to be spurned.

There are many times in an adult's life when autoeroticism is a boon, both in marriage and out of it, when one has a partner or doesn't have one. For example, in. marriage when one partner is separated from the other, when one partner is sick and the other well, or when one partner has died and the lonely surviving partner has not found another mate or prefers not to marry again. In a way autoeroticism is like a generous insurance policy given us by Mother Nature. Just as we have two hands and two feet and two eyes and two legs and two ears—we are also given several ways of expressing our sexuality. This holds from birth to death, for after all we are sexual creatures from birth to death.

Petting to Orgasm: The Gentle Touch

There is still another form of sexuality which you may appreciate more and more as you begin to develop a deep and involving social relationship with someone of the opposite sex.

When you are eleven, twelve, or thirteen, you may not be at all interested in the opposite sex except as wonderful friends and playmates. But somewhere around fourteen or fifteen or sixteen, you may find yourself romantically drawn to someone "special." If you are a girl, HE may seem like the answer to a maiden's prayer—and if you are a boy, SHE may seem like the center of the universe. Generally these attachments are short-lived, though they can certainly fool you into believing they are the "real thing." But usually they are temporary because you are changing and growing so fast that the center of the universe today may be way out on the outer edge of your world tomorrow.

Yet while it lasts you may be so drawn to each other that it feels like enduring, lifelong love. You can be sure that sex is a large part of the attraction, however. Now there is nothing wrong in that—as long as you don't let your sexuality knock the sense out of you, or let the tail wag the dog as it were. Marriage and other life commitments are years away. What can you do sexually at this point that won't jeopardize your future life or your partner's?

Let's say you have been "going steady" for some time. You trust each other. You are very good friends and have shared many nonsexual experiences that have provided you with good estimates of each other's character. You've kissed and held hands, necked a bit, but now this just doesn't seem to be enough. Your sexuality is bursting for release and fulfillment together.

At this point a thoughtless young man may try to persuade his partner to have sexual intercourse. But, as I said earlier, this is a great mistake—for the reasons I have already listed. I could tell you of a number of other reasons why intercourse is not the most desirable route for the expression of sexuality at this moment, but not one of them would have a thing to do with traditional "morality." In fact, sexual intercourse is simply not the *only* pleasurable sexual satisfaction nor the best training ground for ultimate artistry in sex.

There is a way, however, that intelligent youth may express sexuality which is perfectly safe and perfectly adapted to his or her need. It is called noncoital *petting to orgasm*. The word *coitus* is another name for intercourse. So *noncoital* means sexuality fulfilled without intercourse.

Sophisticated lovers have known about this very satisfying way of sexual expression for centuries, but the average boy and girl is rarely told about it, though many discover it for themselves. However, because of the persistence of folklore that labels intercourse the "only real thing," young people are deluded into thinking that if they are to know the ultimate, they must have intercourse.

Actually, mutual petting to orgasm is likely to be much *more* satisfying for the girl and equally as satisfying for the boy—and it offers both boy and girl a safe and happily complete way to share their physical affection for each other.

Too often when boys and girls don't know about noncoital petting to orgasm, they pet to the point where the boy is absolutely bursting with tension and then the girl "turns off" because she senses that if she allows stimulation to go on any further, she will be "in too deep," and the boy will insist on intercourse. She then pulls away and both of them are horribly frustrated. It is often at this point that they have a fight and break off their relationship. What they could do instead is continue petting until *both* come to orgasm.

Some people may say, "Oh, that's just mutual masturbation," with scorn in their voices. Technically, they are correct, but they miss the spirit entirely. Done with love and mutual concern for the complete satisfaction, each of the other, it is every bit as fulfilling as sexual intercourse, and often is *more* so.

Married lovers also carry on this kind of sexual activity

preliminary to having intercourse, and sometimes even instead of intercourse. Women particularly need the extensive petting of their genital organs to enable them to come to orgasm, and many men find that a woman's hand or her mouth is more skillful and stimulating than her vagina.

If noncoital petting to orgasm is to be successful, boys and girls must be mature enough to provide satisfactory conditions for themselves, and must have accurate knowledge of cause and effect. Furthermore, they must have a firm agreement or contract with each other that their noncoital activity shall not turn into coital activity.

By satisfactory conditions I mean a protected place—and plenty of time without interruption. Your own home, with your parents' full knowledge and consent, along with their trust in your ability to behave responsibly, is the best place. A secluded spot under the stars—far off the beaten track—in Nature's own world is next best.

You must keep firmly in mind this fact:

Semen ejaculated *anywhere near* the vaginal opening can result in pregnancy *even* though there has been no penetration of the vagina. In other words, even though a girl is a virgin, an intact hymen has holes through which menstrual blood and other secretions escape. So if there is seminal fluid on the outer part of her labia or close to the vaginal opening between her legs, sperm can swim up the liquid and into her vagina.

So let the boy's ejaculation take place in the girl's hands, or somewhere other than near her vagina between her legs. Have some Kleenex handy for cleaning up afterwards.

Boys and girls need to learn each other's uniquely individual sexual response pattern, as well as understand the nature of erotic stimulation in general.

He, for example, must understand that the clitoris, not the vagina, is the key to sexual excitation for her, and that it must be well lubricated if his gentle—oh, so gentle—

caressing is to feel pleasurable to her. She must be willing to tell him—indeed *show* him—just how to proceed for the greatest chance of success. This presupposes, of course, that she has previously caressed herself enough to be knowledgeable.

She needs to know how to handle his penis with skill and reverence, never too roughly. She should ask him to show her how he likes to have it caressed. Many lovers like to kiss each other's genitals—and this is perfectly normal. If you will observe dogs, horses, cows, and other mammals, you will see that most of them share with humans this instinctive urge.

Naturally, in humans, if this is to be an aesthetic experience, the genital organs must be kept scrupulously clean. Girls, as well as boys, must learn to push back the foreskin covering (in the girl's case the clitoris; in the boy's case the penis) and wash. Many girls don't realize that the tissue covering the clitoris is mobile and collects body secretions which are smelly when stale and tend to cause the foreskin to stick to the clitoris; and this in turn reduces sexual pleasure.

Massage of the lower back is very much enjoyed by most lovers. There is a good reason for this. The sex nerve center is located there.

No one has to tell a boy or girl that the lips, the neck, the palms of the hands, and the breasts are sexually sensitive, but many young people are very crude in their early attempts to pet. People don't like to be grabbed or "pawed" or pinched. A gentle touch—one that communicates *feeling*, one that caresses—is the touch that melts, not the one that causes a partner to stiffen in defense.

Often it is the very inability of a boy to be tender that drives his girl to resist, which in turn drives him to feel that the only thing that will melt her is intercourse. This is a false conclusion.

Two persons can experience an ecstasy of joy with any kind of sexual touch provided each is sensitively aware of the other and permits the flow of love to result in open and trustful communication.

5 Dating

The Joys and Scares of Getting Along with the Opposite Sex

Dating: When, Where, and How

Boys and girls are drawn to each other as plants to the sun. Each thrives in the presence of the other, for this is one of the natural laws of life. Yet some boys and some girls are afraid to expose themselves to the dating process, feeling that because of their own ineptness no one will be attracted to them.

I well remember a group of fifteen-year-old girls sitting around my fireplace one night chatting about this problem. One asked, "How can a girl ever get a boy to pay attention to her? What do I have to do to have boy friends?" The same question, I might add, is also asked by boys about girl friends.

I suggested to this particular girl that she pick a boy who really attracted her and that she then make a list of qualities which she genuinely admired in him. Next, that she find a way to communicate her approval of these attributes—either directly to the boy himself in casual conversation or via the school gossip. Several months later the same girl asked, "How do you turn it off? That system works almost too well!"

The "system," of course, is simply the time-tested one of providing an atmosphere of approval, which is what all of us thrive on.

Good dating starts in such an atmosphere. Boys feel

that they can reveal themselves to approving girls and vice versa.

Many boys and girls get the erroneous notion that they have to be handsome football heroes or beautiful prom queens to be liked at all, but this is simply not the case.

The person who said, "After the first five minutes looks don't count," was stating a partial but important truth. While looks *do* count to the degree that both boys and girls like to be seen in the company of someone reasonably attractive, whether you are big or little, an athlete or an editor, a prom queen or a bookworm, is relatively unimportant.

What *is* important is your genuine interest in the other person's feelings; your perception of what he or she is thinking and dreaming; your ability to listen and to stimulate honest communication; your development of good sportsmanship; your sense of humor. In other words, if you are someone whom another person can relax and have fun with, you will have friends of both sexes.

Nearly all persons your age feel a bit uncomfortable in their own skins—because during adolescence growth is going on at such a rate that you hardly know what to expect of yourself from day to day, let alone of others. If your friends seem to have more sophistication about it than you do, don't be misled into thinking that they feel any better about themselves than you do.

The best way to find members of the opposite sex whose interests are compatible with yours is through hobby groups. If music is your cup of tea, join the school orchestra; if drama thrills you, get into the drama club; if writing or editing excites you, get on the staff of the school paper or yearbook. Sports of all sorts are always good for friends.

Don't let your own inexperience stop you. Everyone is a beginner at some time, and you don't have to excel to make friends. Indeed, if you frankly state that you need some help in getting started (rather than pretending to know it all), you are likely to draw the interest of someone who would like to teach you—and thus a new friendship is made.

Your local church may have a youth group—generally meeting on a weekend evening. These groups decide on their own activities, and they can include a wide range, from ice skating to seminars on nearly everything that interests members. The programs are likely to be open-ended, flexible, and fun. And they have three additional advantages: (1) Your parents will approve of your going. (2) The youth leader in charge of the meeting is likely to be a warm-hearted, fun-loving man or woman who will help you make friends and will know how to minimize any problems of shyness you may have. And (3) the other boys and girls want what you want—fun and the intimacy of shared friendship.

Since I have mentioned youth leaders, this might be a good time to mention chaperones in general. The idea may sound old-fashioned or like inviting in the police force to monitor your leisure-time activities. It isn't that way at all. A well-chosen chaperone is a boon and a blessing. A man *and* a woman are preferable—perhaps a young couple close enough in age to you not to have forgotten how you feel about a lot of things—yet old enough and with enough experience so that they can add finesse to the party. They should be full of good ideas for fun, yet not so aggressive that you don't have a chance to express your own ideas. If they are a couple who love each other, you will find them a model worth watching. They can teach you a lot about man-woman relationships—teaching without preaching.

Furthermore, you will have the feeling of freedom, knowing that things won't get out of hand. Sometimes just one or two older aggressive boys or girls can ruin a project or a party for younger teenagers and can lead them into actions they will be terribly sorry for later. Chaperones can soft-pedal such aggression before it gets out of control.

Also, your parents are much more likely to let you join a group when there is chaperonage—especially when it comes to the matter of transportation. Believe it or not, most intelligent parents are far more afraid of teenage driving accidents than they are of teenage sex accidents, and they have a right to be, for the statistics are gruesome.

Many young teenagers team up with older teenagers who have a driver's license just for transportation's sake —but find that they are in for far more than they bargained for.

You will be better off getting a parent to drive a group of you to and from meetings and parties. On the whole, you'll find that parents enjoy doing this. It gives them the feeling of being good for something besides money and you'll find that many a parent is yearning to be closer to you and your friends as well.

Since I have mentioned the hazard of riding in cars driven by older teenagers, I think in all fairness I ought to add that many older teenagers are very responsible and skillful drivers. You or your parents can easily check any given driver's record. Besides, most people drive the way they do other things. If they are thoughtful of others in general and responsible in general, and have been through a driver-education course, they are likely to be as good a risk as many adults. However, I have heard expert driving instructors say that it takes about five years of experience to develop the kind of judgment that permits one to drive as if it were "second nature." So if younger boys and girls remember that, giving the new driver a chance to pay *full* attention to what he or she is doing, it would reduce the risks enormously.

In your early teens it may be tempting to date older boys or older girls. On the whole, however, you will find it wiser to stay within your own age group. The reason for this is as follows:

Allowing for individual differences, of course, boys develop sexually much faster than girls—though girls develop socially faster than boys. An older boy dating a younger girl is likely to put sexual pressure on her to which she is nowhere near being ready to respond, while an older girl dating a younger boy is likely to put social pressures on him which he simply cannot meet. The younger partner may come away from the experience feeling less than good about himself or herself because, quite naturally, he or she has been less than adequate.

This is a good time to talk about how to say no. When anyone puts pressure on you to act in a way not in accord with your own wishes, it helps to recognize that all of the great persons of this world have had one characteristic in common—namely, the ability when necessary to stand alone, to resist pressure.

This may seem to be asking for more courage than many of you have, but the results are not the isolation and rejection you fear, but a new level of *acceptance*. Curiously, you are usually valued by others as you value yourselves—so if you act in accord with your own nature and needs you will generally find that those near and dear to you will soon respect these.

A simple "Thank you for wanting to make love to me, you have paid me a beautiful compliment, but I am not ready for it" is really all that is needed. You will find that the person worth dating is the one who will patiently understand your situation and respect it while your relationship is developing. The person who must have everything at once is hardly worth worrying about to begin with.

A person who makes an overture of affection toward a

partner, however, deserves an appreciative response that says, in essence, "It is great-hearted of you to ask, but I am not yet sure of my way. Thank you just the same!"

While I have on the whole advised against dating partners much older than you, it is also true that really responsible older boys and girls can be great teachers of younger ones. The crucial issue is: watch out for pressure, whether it be social, sexual, or otherwise.

Dating while baby-sitting is a common practice—but it has its hazards. First, you owe it to your employers to check on whether they are willing to have you divide your attention between their children's needs and your date. Second, it exposes you to pressures that may be hard to handle.

Here it is important to mention again that one essential difference between boys and girls is that boys are urgently wanting release from sexual tension at the age of fourteen or fifteen onward. Most girls of a similar age are content with simple affection—hand-holding, an occasional kiss, an arm-around-the-shoulder kind of intimacy.

Alone in a house in which you cannot have the freedom to introduce social activities such as games, food preparation, dancing, playing the record player, and so on, you are left to sit quietly beside your date simply talking, or playing quiet games which may easily drift into the desire for sexual intimacy. If you share such intimacy in another person's house, you run the risk of the employers' arriving home and exploding with wrath. You have also neglected your job; namely, listening for and being responsible for the care of the children. It is inappropriate to spend time for personal lovemaking when you should be doing your job.

Early in your dating experience a lot of the fun comes from discovering what is attractive to you in the opposite sex and finding out, in turn, what in you is attractive to them. This generally involves comparisons of your own feelings while you are with one person as against when you are with another. Naturally, it involves knowing and exploring the personalities of a number of persons, either one at a time or mingling in groups. It is, in fact, perfectly fascinating to discover how the presence or absence of just one person may make a group come alive, be more sensitive to each other or feel more joy in life. You may enjoy reading a book called *Joy* by William Schutz in which the author describes the elements of open, honest communication which results in joyousness not only between the sexes but between all persons.

Young people—and some older people too—who like forthrightness and honesty from each other often mask their deepest feelings behind a shell. Shells are not very intriguing and nothing exciting gets born from a shell. What is intriguing and infinitely rewarding is the exposure of the real self. I know that you will say that this is easier said than done. You are right. For psychological armor is never formed unless at some time in our lives we were scared that something dreadful would happen to us if we didn't hide our feelings. Perhaps we were laughed at or punished for an honest expression of feeling and the resultant misery made us back away from further expression.

So, yes, it does take courage, but this kind of courage is always rewarded by a deepening sense of feeling alive, feeling loved rather than isolated. Gradually, you learn to express feelings in ways that don't incur either wrath or ostracism—but do bring you friendship. Exposure of the self and a willingness to share that self with others is indeed what draws people together in friendship. Out of such friendships come the truly enriching dating relationships which may one day culminate in an attraction and a trust so great that it will lead you into intimacy of mind, body, and soul.

Sex and Seduction: Pressures to "Give In"

There is a difference between sexual expression that grows out of love based on mutual trust and sexual expression that grows out of one partner's lust, though at first it may be hard to make the distinction.

It is especially hard when you think you love your partner, for then you tend to assume your partner loves you, and that your mutual love blesses and sanctifies whatever sexual intimacy he or she wants.

Frequently, however, these sexual feelings are nothing more and nothing less than simply *sexual feelings*. Not that there is anything wrong with sexual feelings—far from it—but it can be heartbreaking to confuse these with love and to base your actions on a false premise.

This is just where young people often get hurt. Sexual pressure, crying for release, can lead one partner—most often a boy—to make extravagant *protestations* of love which he hasn't the slightest notion of following through by later *acts* of love.

Yet need for assurances of love can seduce the other partner—most often a girl—into nearly any kind of sexual activity he proposes.

Later, when it is discovered that sex alone—not love —was talking, the seduced partner grows bitter and may begin to hate and distrust the opposite sex, which is a pity.

Learn early to recognize sex pressure—both in yourself and in others. If you, either as a boy or as a girl, can be aware of your own sexuality and sense that it is getting ahead of the other aspects of your relationship with a given individual, go cautiously. Autoeroticism or a deliberate concentration on some highly enticing nonsexual activity, can relieve the pressure.

Learn to use such pressure-relieving devices while you give yourself time to establish a relationship of intimacy that can be trusted on levels other than sex. Remember that all love contains sex, but not all sex contains love. The more nonloving the sex may be, the more the seductive pressure may become—and this, in any language, is sheer coercion.

Coercion is trouble.

When two people really trust and love each other, no coercion is necessary. Their sexual expressiveness is always thoughtful of the other's well-being even to the point of giving up their own pleasure, should such a gift benefit the beloved.

Many men and some women believe that, if they can get a partner a bit drunk or a little high on marijuana, sexuality will be appreciably more accessible. Actually, sexuality and alcohol are poor mixers. Alcohol is a depressant, and while one drink may loosen a person's inhibitions, many drinks may make a man not only impotent but a very poor lover, and may make a woman either sleepy, sick, or not very responsive or responsible. In any event, the aftermath of sex and alcohol is likely to be less than exhilarating. Any act entered into without one's whole consciousness will leave the participant feeling sheepish, less than good about himself or herself. Sex especially is marvelous to the degree to which one is consciously *with* it, not blocked off from it through the haze of alcohol.

This also holds true for marijuana and for other "mind-expanding" drugs. Sex itself is expanding and depends for its ecstasy on the full conscious powers of the imagination and the senses. Anything that distorts the mind or the senses instead of bringing them into sharp focus upon the delights of sex *lessens* the power of sex rather than increases it.

There is a lot of discussion these days about aphrodisiacs. An aphrodisiac is supposed to be a food or a substance which when imbibed will make a person feel more sexy or will heighten his or her sexual powers.

There has been a worldwide search for an aphrodisiac that would really work. Thus far none have been discovered which stand the test of science. Nevertheless, dozens of substances have been proclaimed to have aphrodisiac qualities, but you can discount all the proclamations—at least for the present.

The power of the imagination is the greatest aphrodisiac, which is why pornography is so popular for some lovers. It stimulates the imagination of persons who need a quick and easy boost to their own erotic imaginations.

Ordinarily, pornographic books are written by men— for men—and thus are far more stimulating to males than to females. The ordinary pornographic book portrays a swift succession of erotic sequences in the hope that one of them will strike a responsive chord in the reader and thus stimulate him sexually.

Some pornographers are writing for women; these develop an erotic theme along emotional lines in which, instead of pure action, there is a build-up of emotional tension.

It is my opinion that people in their teens don't need the crutch of pornography to stimulate them. Pornography is really a tool of older lovers who want and need stimulation that isn't forthcoming from their own energy system or their own imaginations.

All kinds of social pressure to engage in sex before you feel ready to is something that most of you are going to have to face at one time or another. Many young people kiss good night when they no more feel like kissing than they feel like landing on the moon. Each thinks that the other expects it when in truth it would have been much more fun to have simply said, "Bye, good night, and thank you for a good time."

Perhaps if you are lucky and wise, you will learn to trust your own inner time clock for the natural expression of your growing love for any individual. Like a bud bursting in spring, it will emerge following, not preceding, many other acts that demonstrate love.

6 Sensual Versus Sexual

Good Body Feelings—With a
Little Help from Your Friends

When you were little you got a lot of cuddling and you thrived on it. Indeed, small babies depend so much on stroking of their skin that if they are seriously deprived, they may even die.

If you have ever watched a mother cow with her newly born calf, you will have noticed that she isn't satisfied until that calf is on its feet and nuzzling away at her teats. If the calf is sluggish she licks it with her tongue until she has gotten it interested in suckling. The same is true of a mother dog with her puppies. Stroking them with her tongue, she stimulates their skin surfaces almost as if she were saying, "Come on! Get up and live. Living is good!"

And life *is* good when we experience pleasurable stimulation of any part of our bodies. In fact, all over our bodies are nerve endings reporting pleasure back to our brains. When our backs are rubbed or our faces stroked, we like it and want more. Boys and girls in our summer camp like it so much that often, in the evening while a counselor is telling a story, the campers sit in a big circle, each one rubbing the back of the person in front of him or her.

We speak of such pleasure as "sensual pleasure." Many adults have denied themselves and their children sensual activities for fear that these will lead to sexual intercourse. This can indeed occur. However, sensual pleasure can also be so satisfying in itself that what it more generally leads to is a deep feeling of relaxation and a sense of emotional closeness.

I believe that all people, adults and children alike, need much more of this kind of experience, if for nothing other than healthy release of tension and the generation of feelings of tenderness. But sadly, in our culture, the older a child grows the less of body cuddling and stroking he or she generally gets, and the more of bodily "discipline," which feels the very opposite of affectionate caring. A dirty child is often brusquely scrubbed and also told not to dawdle in the bath; clothes are sometimes jerked on and off impatiently, with none of that delicious "time for play" that was part of "bath-time for baby." Sometimes there is a poke on the fanny to hurry Johnny off to school, where he may be roughly grabbed on the shoulder to marshal him into line.

Just as your body craved pleasurable attention when you were a baby, it continues to crave it all through your life and you will do almost anything to get it. It would be a very good thing indeed if everyone, from kindergarten on, were taught how to massage and touch others in pleasurable ways. It would provide not only delightful, life-giving sensory experience, but could help bring about that sense of closeness to another human being which is so important to all, especially in those years between ten and fifteen when your bodies may be giving you a lot of confusing messages about yourselves.

You could, of course, initiate this nice state of affairs for yourself by learning to rub backs, and by doing it now and then for your friends. In turn they would probably begin doing it for you, and soon you would have developed a small group of intimates on whom you could count for this kind of nourishment.

Backs seem to collect tensions of all sorts and it is wonderful to have these massaged away by healing hands. Just behind your shoulders, up near the base of your neck, are what I call "the mad muscles." They are the muscles that go into tension every time you want to strike out to hit someone. Everyone feels like hitting, throwing, kicking, scratching, screaming, or biting when frustrated or angry. But each of us learns to curtail those actions, and what we do instead is to tense the muscles that want to go into action. If these muscles are held too tightly for too long a time, they go into spasm instead, and we experience what most of us are fairly familiar with—sore shoulders—and we "ouch" if anyone so much as touches us at the point of spasm.

Some people learn fairly early that one way to get rid of such tension is to punch or kick something soft, like a pillow or a mattress, or to throw a ball around, or play a game like tennis or golf. Another way is to lie on a nice soft mattress and bang your arms and legs up and down like a two-year-old having a tantrum—and yell (if you are in a place where you can yell without bringing down the house). Then when you are out of breath, just lie there and sigh deeply. While you are exhaling, letting all the air out of your lungs and collapsing your chest, get a friend to press gently on your "mad" muscle. Chances are that the spasm will break in a second and you'll feel wonderfully relaxed. After that you are ready to bask in a massage of your shoulders and neck.

If you cannot find anyone who knows how to release the initial spasm, don't worry—just bang your own arms up and down on a couch for a few moments, which will dispel any stored up "anger" tensions and then ask a friend to rub your back.

If you are doing the rubbing, start with some nice long strokes of the whole back. If you apply pressure, apply it on the upstroke. It is also nice to use baby oil or some other lubricant that will allow your hands to slip over the skin easily. Round off your strokes in a kind of circular movement so that your partner doesn't feel any jerkiness (which is jarring to the nerves). Try always to keep at least one hand in contact with your friend's body, for if you remove all body contact during a massage, your partner will feel a real break in emotional contact with you and will suffer a sense of isolation at a time when he or she was just relaxing into a state of "trust" and the secure feeling of being cared for by a friend.

When you have rubbed the whole back for a few minutes, try massaging just the shoulders. You can usually apply quite a little pressure with your thumbs, moving them in a circular motion, starting near the spine (though not on it) and moving in circles that end just over the tip of the shoulder.

If you get the least bit serious about becoming proficient at massage, I suggest you get a book like The Massage Book by George Downing and really study it. It is written very clearly and simply and has lots of helpful illustrations. Massage is an art very much worth your time to learn. I can promise you that you will find yourself in demand when your friends discover that you have educated hands that can make their backs or heads or feet feel good.

Here is something else you should know about the back—in relation to tensions. Just above the kidneys is another set of muscles that go into tension, and sometimes into spasm, when a person tries to keep from sobbing. I call them the "sad" muscles. I am sure that you have been told over and over when you've felt like crying, "Stiffen up your spine, boy," or "Buck up and put starch in your spine; big brave boys don't cry." And you have probably tightened that spot in your spine where you would normally break down and sob. Probably you have also "swallowed down" those sobs. Now if this tension isn't released, you may carry it around with you and then wonder why you have a pain in that part of your back. When you get a massage, you may suddenly find youself bursting into tears. This is nothing to worry about—in fact, it is something to rejoice over; for long-held tensions can only mean trouble and to let go of them is a relief. If you are massaging someone else and this happens, all you need do is to acknowledge that it is a good thing to let go of stored sobs, and you can say that you are glad that your friend trusts you enought to "let go" with you. You can also go right on rubbing that place till it feels fully relaxed.

In the very lowest segment of the back are the muscles that connect to our sexual organs. Many people suffer low back pain because they have held in their sexual feelings for so long and so hard. When their lower back is massaged, it often helps them feel wonderful and in contact again with their own good feelings. Sometimes lovers massage each other's lower backs before making love as this seems to melt away any residual tension they may have brought to each other and prepares their bodies for sexual expression. However, massaging a lower back doesn't have to lead to sex. It can lead to very good feeling generally. Women, just before their menstrual periods, are especially grateful for a massage of their lower backs.

Heads, necks, and faces are other areas that feel wonderful when massaged. When you stroke a friend's face, do it very gently. Beginning at the center of the forehead, just above the eyes, let your fingers stroke to the sides of the head, ending each stroke in a kind of circular curlicue behind the ears. Start each stroke about half an inch above the preceding one until the hairline of the forehead has been reached, and then do the whole thing over again several times. Then do it below the eyes until you reach the chin, then stroke upward from the chin to the cheekbones.

If you massage the scalp, use your fingers to move the skin of the scalp, not just the hair. It feels great. Here you can really let your fingertips (not nails) dig in until your friend tells you you are doing it hard enough. You can massage your own face and scalp too.

Some people love to have their feet massaged. In fact, professional masseurs in Japan always begin with the feet, while professional masseurs in Sweden begin with the head. If you do massage your friend's feet, be sure to do it with a firm strong touch or it may feel very ticklish. If your friend's feet are cold when the weather outside isn't cold, you may usually assume that your friend is suffering some anxiety. In fact, many people will say, "I've got cold feet" about something they are afraid of, and if you took their feet in your hands at that moment, you would find that they did indeed have cold feet. If someone you care about is in such a state of anxiety, it is especially reassuring to them to take their feet in your hands and warm them with massage. It is also good to have your own feet massaged after a long hike or after you have been standing on them for many hours.

Place the whole palm of your hand against the flat of their foot and simply warm their foot for a few moments. Then take your thumb and with strong circular movements massage the ball of your friend's foot. Take each toe, starting with the big toe, and stretch it out as far as it will go and then rub it around the base (where it joins the foot). Then take the heel in your hand, and with your other hand massage around it and the lower leg. If your friend complains that you are tickling, just apply greater pressure. It is generally the very light, feathery touch or the nervous touch that is perceived as ticklish.

Actually, tickle spots are usually pleasure spots held in tension. If the tension were totally relaxed, the same stroke that is felt as a tickle would be felt as pure pleasure. On the other hand, if the tension is increased, it will be perceived as pain. Thus it is quite possible that a person could be tortured by being "tickled to death." So make sure that your stroking is firm, relaxing, and truly caring.

Hands also enjoy being stroked. Perhaps hands get more stimulation than most parts of our bodies, however. Certainly people who love each other indulge in more hand holding and hand stroking than in other kinds of body stroking.

I can remember as a small child that one of the things I liked most when sitting next to a favorite aunt was her "playing with" my hands. I could sit patiently through any amount of boring adult chatter as long as she kept on stroking them.

As you grow up you won't get very much stroking from adults. Probably most of the touching you get has to do with controlling you—"do this . . . stop that . . ." You may be lucky in having a parent who still believes in back rubs at bedtime. Even these rubs, however, have probably been discontinued by the time you're an adolescent. There is nothing, though, to keep you from giving your friends massages of the back, head, face, hands, and feet or any other part of them that yearns for attention. And you need not worry that you are being a seducer of the unwilling and unwary. Sexuality is indeed a part of sensuality and vice versa, and lovers regularly use stroking as a prelude to lovemaking. But also remember that stroking is a necessary nutriment to the sense of feeling alive and is usually received as a warming gift of caring. I hope you give your friends this gift as often as you can and I hope they give it to you.

7 Same-Sex Relationships

I like to define sex as energy—a special kind of energy that tends to draw us one to another for companionship, love, physical closeness, body pleasure, and sometimes procreation. When accompanied by feelings of love and trust, sexual energy is one of the greatest powers on earth for releasing that which is good and that which is creative in human beings. When used in an atmosphere of love, earth itself seems to come very close to our concept of heaven. And this is true whether the love we bear is for man, woman, child, nature, or what some people call God.

In twentieth-century America, religion, education, society, and family all impose the view that sexual energy is supposed to move toward a partner of the opposite sex. The fairy stories we imbibe in childhood read that the prince meets the princess; they fall in love, marry, and live happily ever after. This is a great and wonderful myth that most of us grow up believing or wanting to believe. And we can go on believing it (with a few grains of salt), for it does happen to some degree, often enough to be reassuring, despite many failures. As a benign myth it has helped idealize the nuclear family (mother-father-child) as the basic unit of human nurturance.

But sexual energy does not always flow in the direction of man-woman love. Sometimes it is expressed as love of man for man, woman for woman. There are great myths and legends about this kind of loving, too. In ancient Greece, for example, same-sex loving was celebrated as a more elevating experience than love of someone of the opposite sex. So time, history, and social circumstance may make a vast difference as to whether any given population glorifies heterosexual relationships (opposite sex) or homosexual relationships (same sex). As individuals we are sexual beings first and homosexually or heterosexually inclined secondarily, depending to a large extent on our life experience, our hormonal makeup, and the time and place in which we live.

Today, in America, the vast majority of our population considers love between man and woman as the only or most acceptable form of adult love. Yet we also know that thousands upon thousands of happy and productive persons have chosen to focus their love on someone of the same sex. And probably the majority of all people find that they deeply love persons of both sexes (bisexual), and that this love carries with it sexual feeling, expressed or unexpressed.

In the past, moralists, and even some doctors and social scientists, have tended to treat homosexuality as a sickness—to be stamped out or "cured." Homosexuality is not a sickness—though it does place the person making such a choice on the periphery of social acceptance, and this in itself can lead to feelings of isolation and rejection which certainly do not make for emotional health. Without the effects of that isolation, however, the person choosing a lover of the same sex is no more "sick" or "well" than his or her heterosexual brothers and sisters. But he or she may be subject to a great deal of pressure to change. Often he (or she) does change, directing his or her sexual love life into the common stream of what we choose to call "normality." Many persons choose not to change, however, either because they have truly found the love of their lives in a person of their own sex and would no more give up that love than heterosexual lovers would renounce their love, or they are, indeed, emotionally and physically stuck and can *only* move homosexually.

In the instance of true love, I hope that we will someday recognize the sanctity of these unions and honor and protect them, just as we honor and protect our heterosexual unions.

In the instance of people who are stuck, we need to understand what makes anyone get stuck in a form of behavior, especially one that affects something as profound as sexuality.

Let's take a look at how most of us are brought up and see if this sheds any light on our sexual leanings.

Almost all of us, to begin with, are given a chance to know someone of our same sex far sooner than someone of the opposite sex. Little girls (and big girls) are permitted intimacies with other girls, and boys are permitted intimacies with other boys that would never be permitted between boys and girls. Girls, for example, are allowed to spend the night and to sleep in the bed of another girl, and likewise boys. But girls are not permitted in the beds of boys. It is as normal as apple pie for an affectionate and adventurous child to reach out to hug, stroke, cuddle, and maybe discover sexual pleasure with his or her intimate bedfellow. Some will discover the first strong feelings of attachment and sexual love.

In all the nonsexual areas of their lives also, girls are thrown in with girls, and boys with boys, more than with each other. In their choice of studies in school, there is a strong predetermination of what they are directed to focus on (such as shop for boys and homemaking for girls), though fortunately this sexism is slowly disappearing.

Because they are thrown together so continuously, girls tend to admire, and sometimes to adore, other girls.

The same is true of boys. Sometimes the adoration takes on many of the characteristics of an infatuation (just as the first strong attraction between boys and girls or men and women also may be infatuation).

This does not invalidate the experience, however. Love is love at whatever level it shows itself. It may not be lasting love, but if its major characteristic is a true caring for the well-being of the beloved, it deserves respect and whatever time it may take to discover if this is an enduring part of one's life or a passing phase. The chances are on the side of its being a passing phase, but not always.

What about the person who feels stuck, who wants to move on to a heterosexual relationship, or at least to include a heterosexual relationship in his or her life but feels that he or she cannot or is paralyzed by the experience when he or she comes close to it? Or why do some persons who have loved a person of their own sex refuse to expand their love potential to include heterosexual love? In other words, what causes "fixed" homosexuality in a world in which the pressures are all in the other direction?

The causes are probably many, and not entirely known or understood, even by those professionals who claim to be experts in the field.

Some counselors feel that when a girl has been browbeaten by her father, or a boy has been psychologically castrated by his mother, they turn from the opposite sex, seeking loves from among their own sex whom they feel are more trustworthy.

Other counselors feel that when there is no father image in a home, a boy will search for a loving man in his life—and that a girl will search for a loving woman if she has in some way been deprived of a mother.

There is also a theory that some boys and some girls are simply born with a hormonal "imbalance," which forms a biologic basis for their tendency to gravitate to members of their own sex. This group would represent what Dr. Alfred Kinsey (who was one of the early great sex researchers) called a 6. He had classified people on a scale from 0 to 6, in which 0 represented those who had never had or wanted to have any homosexual experience and 6 those having nothing but homosexual experience. The 5s and 6s had very little interest in or ability to direct their sexual expression into heterosexual channels. In fact, when some of them, under social pressure, sought psychologic help to do so, they found themselves utterly miserable. I think that most psychologists agree today that these individuals are far happier when they continue to seek their love life from among persons of their own sex.

The vast majority of people, being both sexual *and* capable of love, can love either a man or a woman, or both. What determines their choice is largely who it is that crosses their paths at a time when they are open for love, plus the strong pressures that society exerts to limit lovemaking to someone of the opposite sex. In this, as in other things, it takes a brave and committed person to do something that society frowns on, and our society, at least, has certainly frowned on homosexuality.

This attitude is relaxing, however. The unfairness of condemning a man or a woman because they have chosen to love someone of their own sex is becoming more and more obvious to rational human beings. But most of us are far from rational. We react out of emotional habit patterns induced at very young ages. If we have been told that there is something terribly wrong about making love to someone of our own sex before we have lived long enough to examine this thesis carefully, we absorb it (just as for centuries people accepted that the world was flat). Then, when we feel a perfectly normal attraction to some-one of our own sex, we get scared that something is wrong with us—that we are "abnormal." Sometimes we get so scared that we lean over backward in the other direction, even to the extent of launching an attack on anyone who appears to be the least bit "queer" or "that way." You can pretty well guess that the rabid denouncers of homosexuals are those who themselves feel such a strong pull in the direction of homosexual activity (whether they're aware of it or not) that in order to control these impulses in themselves, they fight them unreasonably in others.

Because of the very viciousness of these attackers, several organizations have formed to protect the social and legal rights of those who choose to live their lives as homosexuals. These groups also act as social clubs where couples can mingle without being pointed out as off-beat from the rest of society. Incidentally, persons in enduring homosexual partnerships are not the phonies one sees on the street masquerading as male-female teams parading their "differentness"; not the "butches" and "queens," not those on the prowl for a quick "blow job," not a same-sex prostitute or pimp. Such sexual behavior does come under the heading of "sick"—is often exploitative and has nothing to do with loving.

Older women—those in their seventies and eighties—outnumber men of that age three to one. Furthermore, the few available men in this oldest bracket tend to seek out much younger women, if they do seek a marital partner at all. So some older women are learning to seek each other, discovering that they need not live out a lonely old age without companionship or sex.

You, of course, being young, are more interested in the problems of your own age—so let us return to these. If you as a young person find yourself in love with someone of your same sex, what should you do about it? Will you be afraid and pull away from the relationship because of your fear of social disapproval? Or will you embrace it and live it for whatever value it has for you? Will you deny the reality of sexual undercurrents that tug at you from time to time, or will you accept that they exist and allow yourself to move as close to or as far away from a friend of the same sex as you might, in similar circumstances, move in relation to someone of the opposite sex?

It is difficult to offer advice in such situations and often the solutions are not simple. Sometimes you can have a love experience with a person of your own sex and also, at the same time, have a wonderful relationship with someone of the opposite sex. These instances are rare and involve very mature and liberated persons. More often you can have a love relationship with someone of your own sex in adolescence and later consummate a wonderful love with someone of the opposite sex. In fact this is fairly common. Another solution, and probably the one most often practiced, is to enjoy a deep and warm friendship with someone of the same sex—but without direct sexual expression—and channel all of your sexual love toward someone of the opposite sex. This solution gets the most support from society.

One thing that I am very glad to see happening in our culture is the freeing of boys to walk arm in arm with each other and to engage in gestures of affection. Males in most other places in the world have always been allowed the pleasure of embracing each other on meeting, even in some instances of kissing each other—such as fathers and sons. But in our country, until the present, boys were taught to stand rigidly away from each other, with only the formal handshake for greeting. This overemphasis on the sexual implications of male touching has tended to focus many a man's attention on sex when his real need and his honest feeling was for exchange of affection. Today boys do hug each other and they are not necessarily called "fags" or "queers." The enjoyment they can experience in body closeness may help them to enjoy spiritual closeness which, in turn, may help them to become more loving human beings.

Fortunately, girls have always been permitted to hug and kiss each other to some extent. I hope they will continue to do so, for both boys and girls (and men and women) miss something important to balance out their lives if they do not enjoy the affection of someone of their own sex, as well as love of someone of the opposite sex.

8 Sex and Your Family

"My Parents Would Die if They Knew"

Your mother and your father probably care more about your well-being than anyone else you will ever know until you find a committed lover. Sometimes it may not seem so to you, especially when it comes to sex. On this topic they may be either noncommunicative or even actively negative and hostile. Even if they do seem to have a good feeling about sex, their past training may have been such that they learned to soft-pedal talking about it—so drastically that you may be unaware that they ever enjoyed sex at all.

Educating Your Parents

In any case, a logical conclusion you might be justified in drawing is either that sex is fearful (too fearful to talk about) or that it is one of those goodies adults reserve for themselves and therefore taboo for you. However, you'd be wrong on both counts. Sex is neither fearful nor taboo nor reserved for adults and, furthermore, I don't believe that most enlightened parents want to insulate you from its positive aspects. At least those whom I know don't. Some, however, are embarrassed and some are afraid that you'll get hurt. Others simply don't know how to talk about it, because they never learned how from *their* parents. You may even be the first generation in your family in which adults didn't think it positively dangerous for young people to have *any* knowledge of sex at all, let alone to act upon it.

It was only a few years ago that sexual knowledge was equated with evil. "Good little boys and girls" were supposed to know nothing until they were married. And then, by some magic which rarely happened, they were supposed to fall blissfully into their wedding beds. Few found it blissful—especially the women. Your parents, who possibly were subjected to that experience, may have many painful memories that they'd like to forget. Also, studies show that about one-third of all adult women today have been pregnant before their marriage—and that wasn't very easy to live through either. Your parents don't want that to happen to you. Part of their reticence lies in their fear that if they talk too freely and positively with you, you may be tempted to experiment too early with intercourse—and with the wrong persons. In short, they fear you will get hurt. Then, mistakenly, instead of helping you to become skillful and safe and joyous in your experience of sex, they simply tell you "don't"—often with a lot of scary admonitions. And of course you very shortly get the idea that sex is something you can't discuss openly with your parents. It is just a bombshell that gets you nothing but your parents' wrath (for fear, you may know, often masquerades as anger).

Nevertheless, and in spite of fear (maybe even because of it), most parents want you to have both information and positive attitudes about sex, and in their heart of hearts they want you to have safe enjoyment of it. They may, however, be finding it hard to communicate with you about it, and this may be partly because of your own silence on the subject. They may have given you a book on sex in the hope that it will open up conversation between you. It would be a help if you would ask some questions sometimes so that they could have openings for discussion.

Sex educators today are trying to help parents to talk

with their children. They are especially trying to help them see that all of us are sexual beings from birth to the grave, and that there is some satisfying and ethical way to experience sexuality at every age and stage of life. They are also helping parents to discover the resources in their community that will aid their boys and girls.

Every time I am involved in a seminar for young people on the subject of sex, the one most frequent request I get is, "Please talk to our parents and help them to talk to us without our getting the feeling that we're bad if we want to discuss our sexuality with them. And please try to persuade them that if we want to be alone in our rooms with a member of the opposite sex, it is because we want to know each other intimately and privately and we are not going to get pregnant."

Let's divide these two requests into two parts—the talking and the doing.

When you say that you'd like to "talk" with your parents, you are really saying that you want to share with them (and have them share with you) feelings about sexuality as well as facts. You're too big for the agricultural approach (how babies are made—you probably learned about all that in kindergarten). Now in your teens you want affirmation of your own feelings and you want to hear from those with experience as to how sexuality can be expressed in satisfying ways and with no bad consequences. Who better to talk with than your parents!

But before either you or your parents can talk productively, you will both have to understand certain historic phenomena that are brand new in the world, and cannot help but deeply influence all sexual action in ways that are very different from any previous time in history.

First, the old biblical injunction "to be fruitful and multiply" is no longer an ethical command. As every schoolboy or girl now knows, the world does not need a larger population. In fact, it needs great restraint in the production of babies. Having a child is a matter for serious, thoughtful consideration, to be undertaken only when you can be fully responsible for its care. Furthermore, the technology for limiting childbirth exists in a near-to-perfect state for the first time in our evolution. Every human being over the age of puberty has to learn this technology, whether he or she is married or not married, if he or she is to participate responsibly in sexual intercourse with anyone of the opposite sex. Ninety-nine percent of all sexual activity will not be for the production of babies—in marriage or out. Let us admit from the start that our sexuality is primarily for pleasure and for communion with another human being. Only a few times in any person's lifetime will it be for procreation.

Second, young people today mature physically several years earlier than did their parents. Not so long ago fifteen was the average age at which girls menstruated for the first time. Today it is at age twelve. Also, young persons today marry several years later than did their grandparents. In grandmother's time the average age was eighteen. Today the average age is twenty-two. What all this means is that the transition stage from childhood to the assumption of full adult marital status is extended from just two or three years to a lengthy ten or twelve years. No one, not even the most avid puritan, could expect anyone, young or old, to lay away in cold storage his or her sexuality for as long as that. It could lead to more harm in terms of sexual and emotional dysfunction than some of the other consequences that have caused parents to fear sexual expression ever did.

Talking About Sexuality

The real questions that you and your parents have to talk about are how, when, where, and with whom you *are* going to express your sexuality, along with an airing of your feelings and theirs.

Obviously, the best place for anyone to express his or her sexuality is in the privacy and safety of his or her own home. This involves an attitude on both your part and your parents' that sex is good—not just to be tolerated as an idea, but actively experienced as good. Sex may be very private, but it is not a secret to be hidden from other members of the family. Just as your mother and father enjoy the privacy of their own bedroom, you might ask for the privacy of yours.

Some parents respond to such an idea with "If I give my child that privilege, I will be condoning sex." And this is the truth. They will be condoning sex. But sex, as you'll remember, has been declared good, not bad; private, but not secret. Some parents have said that they wouldn't mind having their adolescent boy or girl have the privacy of their own bedrooms in which to entertain their friends, but how explain the closed door to the younger children in the house. How indeed! How explain anyone's need for privacy—one of the essentials of life in these complex and overcrowded times. Here is where an adult's positive (or negative) attitude toward sex shows up most. Here they have to "put their money where their mouth is," or else acknowledge to themselves and to their children that sex is *not* good after all (which they know to be a patent lie). If they are reasonable and open they can come to feel, as well as *want* to feel, that sex, in some form, is for everyone—even their children.

Perhaps you could direct their thinking a bit by asking questions like these: "Do you think that infants are sexual? When they 'play' with themselves, do you think they get pleasure? Did I play 'doctor' games when I was little? Did you nurse me? Did you enjoy it? How did kids manage masturbation when you were young? How old were you when you had your first boy friend (girl friend)? Did you pet with him (her)? Did you come to orgasm through petting, or did you feel you had to stop once your feelings got aroused? How do you feel about mutual petting to orgasm now without intercourse?"

It is important to choose a time and a place that are appropriate for sexual discussion, for example when your parents are feeling good toward each other and toward you. Try expressing what your own feelings are, and state positively what kind of help you would like from them, letting them know what they can expect from you.

If you meet with a solid wall of resistance, you might tell them that you do understand, but that you'd like it a lot if they would read some of the books listed in the bibliography of this book. Or ask them to go to some of the parents' meetings about sexuality that are being held by many churches today. Or get them to talk with other parents whom you know to be more positive about sex than your own are.

Of course, you don't say, "Why don't you be more like Lisa's mother," which would only make your own mother furious. Instead you might say (a bit wistfully), "Lisa tells me that she and her parents have wonderful talks together about their sexual feelings. I wish we could."

It is just possible that your mother might then open up and ask, "What about sex would you like us to talk about?" Then you'd have to brave it and acknowledge that you do have a lot of sexual feeling that you don't entirely know what to do with; that you masturbate, which helps a lot, but that you also want to pet with John and that you want to do it safely and in the privacy of your own room.

Your mother might balk at first, but then again she might not. At any rate, when she has thought about it a bit, she may see that your request is sensible.

Parents, when they have given your emerging sexuality some thought, have no objection whatsoever to your having positive sexual experiences. What they resist is your flaunting sexuality as if it were a new and threatening toy, your indiscretions of speech or action in front of their conservative friends, or your waving your new-found sexual prowess under the noses of younger brothers or sisters whom they, your parents, don't feel are ready to confront the scene of you and your boy friend petting naked. Nor do they want you to have any unpleasant scenes with the police by petting in a parked car, and they may be even more fearful of a hurtful encounter with bands of roving ruffians who attack young couples petting in parks, parked cars, or other public places.

Their first protective instinct is to say, "don't" rather than "how-to." It is up to you to help them find ways to say "yes," and "how" without antagonism developing between you. One of the worst things that happens between teenagers and their parents is for both to "polarize." This means that one starts the process by taking an extreme position. This tends to force the other to take an equally extreme and untenable position in the opposite direction. Here they both freeze—and never the twain shall meet— and the situation seems hopeless.

Avoid this possibility if you can. Ask questions that can be answered by *when, where, how*—not by *yes* or *no*. Don't ask, "Why not?" or "Why?" Most people don't know why or why not, and these words only send them up a wall. "Tell me about it" or "Will you explain more about your position" are better approaches.

Don't start a rebuttal of your parents' position with the word *but*. Acknowledge their position with as much positive consideration as you can muster. You might say, "I see your point of view. Thank you for sharing it with me. Now I am wondering if you can see mine, along with some of the changes that are occurring in my life and in the lives of my friends."

The same principle of communication about sexuality

(or about any other meaningful or controversial subject) works with other adults as well as with your parents and, incidentally, with persons of your own age as well.

Don't diminish or downgrade the other person's point of view or try to make him (or her) feel smaller or more insignificant than he or she is. Yet do acknowledge your own feelings. Preface a statement of feeling by the words "I feel—," thus taking responsibility for your own feelings. No one can argue the authenticity of *your* feelings. They can only argue with you if you try to "put a trip on them" by saying, "You make me feel—" or "Don't you think—."

One thing that teenagers have a hard time understanding is the sexual feeling many fathers have for their daughters and mothers have for their sons. These same mothers and fathers have been told that such feelings are taboo; so when they feel them just the same, they tend to pull away, to withdraw from the nice, cuddly, affectionate things they've done with you in the past. Some become overstrict and negative about all kinds of sensuous experience. It might help if you understood this possibility so that when Daddy pushes you out of his lap with a gruff "You're too big for this sort of thing," you won't get your feelings hurt or believe that he doesn't love you anymore, or rush out and throw yourself into the arms of the first boy you meet just to prove to yourself that someone loves you. Your daddy still loves you, all right. You can be sure of that, but he may be afraid of his own sexual feeling for you and he may, on the one hand, tell you you're too big for lap holding or cuddlings, and, at the same time, try to keep you "his little girl" by "protecting" you from the boys who "just want to exploit you."

There are boys who exploit, of course, and girls too— and you'll just have to learn the difference between the takers and the givers. This isn't really so difficult, after all, and depends on trusting your own feelings.

There is also a tasteful way of doing everything, and

sexuality is no exception. Good taste is generally based on consideration of the feelings of those with whom you are in contact. In sexual feeling, you may feel so wonderfully good, floating as if you needed heavy weights to hold you down, that it is very easy to gloat and let the whole world know of your happiness. Unfortunately, there are a lot of people who can't stand happiness in others. You can generally tell them by their dried-up appearance, by their aloofness in the face of joy. Such persons can be really hurtful; so it is well that you learn early to avoid sharing your exuberances with them. In fact, it is generally a very good idea to look carefully at the emotional state of anyone with whom you want to share any kind of feeling. It is part of good taste—and sensitivity—to notice where the other person "is," and if he or she is in a position to "hear" you with an open heart. If not, wait until a riper time. This too is part of growing up—learning to wait a bit until conditions are "right" before barging in.

⑨ Sex Language
Sacred and Profane

How you feel about something is often influenced by the language used to talk about it. This works another way as well—how you feel about something determines how you talk about it. Sex is no exception. Every sexual act, every sexual process, every sex-related part of the body has acquired two sets of terms, one stemming from human beings who feel that sex is good, beautiful, and worthy, and the other from those who feel that sex is essentially bad, dirty, shameful, and to be ridiculed.

Scientists, poets, lovers (young and old) generally are at the former end of the scale. Repressed moralists, ignorant guttersnipes, and those who try to be funny at someone else's expense generally are at the latter. Somewhere in between are the vast majority of people who haven't sorted out their feelings or who may be embarrassed by the language of lovers and so resort to slang, or who, in general, use words indiscriminately with no thought of their effect upon others. One summer at our children's summer camp we had some campers like that. They punctuated every sentence with the words *fuck* and *shit* as if they were commas, till the words themselves ceased to have any meaning. We started a class in "creative cursing" just to provoke them into thinking about what they were saying and choosing the words they *wanted* for appropriate occasions.

Shakespeare did that, by the way, immortalizing his

"seven classic four-letter words," but he used these with utmost care to portray his characters as he wanted them portrayed. (These are, by the way, *shit*, *fuck*, *fart*, *cunt*, *cock*, *piss*, and *arse*.)

Profanity has its place when we want to relegate something to the gutter, ridicule it, let off negative steam, or we simply have explosive energy that has nowhere else to go.

But if you want to express tenderness or reverence for something, or raise it in your consciousness, you use language that inspires these feelings. For example, if someone says "he pawed me," the listener receives a very different message than if the speaker had said "he caressed me."

One of the sad things in our culture is that many people have heard the gutter words, the crude words for sexuality long before they have heard either the correct scientific words or the beautiful phrases an educated and sensitive lover uses with his or her beloved. Then their whole attitude about sex is warped by the language of coarseness. Actually, there are no dirty sexual acts between persons who care for each other, and certainly no shameful parts of the body. There are only dirty words to describe sexual acts and sex-related parts of the body.

One of the special cruelties of language, and one that has again and again been repudiated by women, has to do with men calling a woman by a part of her body, such as "a piece of ass." Her whole personality is thus relegated to the dimensions of a sex object.

I have never heard women do this to men, except recently in response to such a denigration—and then I have heard them exclaim, "What a prick he is!"

Such language is not a way to win friends and influence people—especially not a way to woo a woman or make a man feel good about himself.

Once when I was on a television program dealing with sexuality, a woman in the audience asked me what I thought was the value to a woman of sexual intercourse.

My answer was that this depended entirely on whether she was made love to or simply "fucked." The questioner got the point without further elaboration.

"Making love" implies creating an atmosphere between lovers in which each reaches out to the other, expands in the other's presence, shares the best of the self with the other, cares about the other's well-being and happiness.

"Fucking" implies a mechanical or angry act, with or without joy, caring, or consideration. In the act of "making love" lovers feel cherished. In the act of "fucking" they "use" and sometimes feel misused.

Or let's take the word *masturbate*. Actually, *masturbate* is a perfectly correct word for a specific sexual act, but it is a word that denigrates the act—makes it into something less than good because of the roots of the word itself. (As I explained earlier, *masturbate* stems from two words that mean "pollute with the hand.") No wonder that other and coarser slang phrases have become associated with it, like *jerk off* or *beat the meat*, for example. *Autoeroticism* or *self-pleasuring*, on the other hand, imply a tender regard for the self, a caressing touch that brings about pleasure. It is easy to say, "I caressed myself to orgasm" and to feel very good about oneself while making such a statement. But to say, "I masturbated" can turn the very same act into something a bit shame-filled.

Let's take a look at some of the more commonly used slang words relating to sex. Read the first column and notice how you feel about the subject. Then read the second column and note your feelings again. (This is a very partial list of course. You can add many more from your own experience.)

Slang	Scientific or Lover's Language
boobs ⎫ tits ⎭ ————	breasts

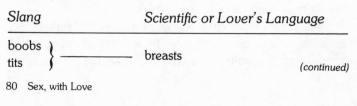

(continued)

Slang	Scientific or Lover's Language
cherry ———————	hymen
paw ⎫ make out ⎬ ——— { feel up ⎭	pet caress stroke
fuck ⎫ screw ⎪ ball ⎬ ——— { hump ⎭	make love have sexual intercourse become one with another sleep together
beat the meat ⎫ masturbate ⎪ jerk off ⎬ — { cream off ⎭	autoeroticism; pleasure myself self-gratification play with myself caress myself to orgasm
beaver ⎫ mouse ⎪ pussy ⎪ cunt ⎬ ——————— vagina hole ⎪ slit ⎪ snatch ⎭	
piece of ass ⎫ a good lay ⎬ ——————— a woman regarded as a sexual object whore ⎪ chick ⎭	
cock ⎫ ——————— penis prick ⎭	
blow job ⎫ go down on ⎪ eat pussy ⎬ ——————— oral lovemaking suck off ⎭	
arse ⎫ ass ⎬ ——————— { bum ⎭	buttocks bottom

(continued)

Slang	Scientific or Lover's Language
fart ————————	making gas
an old fart dirty old man } ——— {	also used to describe a man who is sexually interested beyond what is considered by the speaker as an appropriate age for sexual interest
crap shit } ————————	bowel movement or, briefly, BM
Lezzie dyke butch queer gay } ———————	Lesbian; female homosexual
hard-on —————	erection
cocksucker gay fag faggot drag queen } ————	male homosexual
balls rocks } ————————	testicles
the curse falling off the roof } — {	menstruation period

Slang, of course, is also a form of communication, and like any other communication it requires agreed-upon meanings. For example, if a rough-and-ready truck driver says to his buddy, "She was some chick" the buddy would be quite clear that his friend intended this as a compliment.

However, if the girl happened to be a cultured self-respecting woman, and she heard this comment about herself, she might consider it a put-down, a relegation of herself to the role of sex object, and would not be pleased at all.

You might ask yourself if you are using slang words about sex to enhance your feelings or to hide from them. You may be afraid to express tenderness or love, or even simple affection, in words with feeling—and then you may resort to slang. Slang becomes a way to avoid risk.

Slang is also a way to let out anger before being able to express love. So many people carry around such an excess of unexploded fury, they have to let some of it out through rough speech before they can allow themselves tender feelings. Perhaps the man who says, "Come on, baby, let's fuck!" or "I'm going to screw you!" has this difficulty.

One of the problems you as growing teenagers may have to grapple with is your parents' own embarrassment in talking with you, which results in their giving you double messages, like this:

"Sex is beautiful. You will enjoy fucking your wife when you are married."

10 ⊙ Sick Sex

Rapists, Molesters, Flashers, Goosers, and Other Deadly Garden Pests

When sex energy goes haywire in a disturbed personality, some very freakish behavior can result. Some of it is harmless, such as a man sashaying down a street in exaggerated imitation of a woman. Other behavior, like rape, is criminal, and very harmful indeed. All acts that force sex upon an unwilling partner are deviant and abnormal. Here are some that you may need to know about.

Rape is probably the worst and the most traumatic to its victims. The violence of forced intercourse, endured by a woman only because of the sheer brute strength of the rapist, who also may have a knife to her throat, is utterly terrorizing and injurious as well. Rightfully, rapists belong behind bars and need rehabilitative therapy.

One of the ways to avoid rape is to stay away from places where it can (and often does) occur—lonely parks after dark, unlighted side streets, unpoliced or questionable areas of cities. Never get in a car with a stranger or let a stranger in your house when you are alone. If someone knocks on the door, talk to him through a locked door no matter how silly or antisocial that seems to you. If he says he needs a phone or some other kind of help, offer to do the phoning for him while he remains outside. If he offers you something or has some other very plausible or appealing reason for seeing you, tell him to come back another time—when your parents are at home—that you simply are not permitted to let strangers in. Not every stranger who comes to the door is a rapist, of course. Probably only a small minority are. However, you cannot afford to take chances. Besides, any well-intentioned man will fully understand your reticence about placing yourself in his hands without introduction or chaperonage and will respect your wishes. If not, you can be very sure he has no good intentions toward you.

Self-operating elevators and hallways in apartment buildings in big cities are also target areas for rapists to lurk in. If you are using a self-operated elevator, make sure it is empty or occupied by several other people; don't get in it alone with only one strange man. If you live in an apartment with a doorman, sometimes it is smart to arrange regularly to telephone him on your house phone just as soon as you have reached your own apartment and alert him that you are safely inside your own door. If you must go about a city alone, wear a police whistle about your neck and carry a small mace gun in your hand—not your purse (it is too late then). Yes, I know that it is illegal to carry a "weapon," but this one may save your life—and rape is also illegal. Remember that you can kick a man in the groin so hard that he may be temporarily "out of commission" long enough for you to run. And run you had better. If you are trapped, make as much noise as you possibly can. It is worthwhile for every girl to learn something about the art of self-defense. In many cities and towns today, there are such courses for girls and women. But even if you haven't learned the fine points of jujitsu, you can scratch and bite. Unless he has a knife or you are a victim of gang rape, you stand a fair chance of making life so unpleasant for him that you may escape. However, you may not.

If you *are* raped, by all means call or go to the nearest rape crisis center in your area at once. Such centers are springing up all over the country and the persons serving them have been trained to know just what steps to take to help you most. They will see to it that you get immediate medical aid. They will treat you sympathetically and not as if *you* were at fault in the whole miserable affair. And of course they will do their best to put steps in motion to catch the rapist.

In the past many women hesitated to report rape because of that shameful attitude on the part of male chauvinist policemen that implied that if a woman was raped it was because she wanted to be and may well have encouraged it. They have even been known to say to victims, "I hope you relaxed and enjoyed it."

No one—but *no one* enjoys rape, except maybe the rapist. Fortunately today (and largely because of the efforts of the Women's Liberation Movement, and because of books like *Against Our Will*, by Susan Brownmiller) rape is recognized for what it is: a crime of a man against a woman and one in which the victim needs sympathy, understanding, medical help, and psychotherapy to overcome its effects. The last thing she needs is a police grilling or a courtroom scene in which she has to prove her innocence.

Child molesters, usually strangers hanging around children's playgrounds or lurking along trails known to be used by children on their way to and from home and park, are criminals just as rapists are criminals. Their target victims, however, are children rather than adult women. Obviously, they can be very dangerous indeed. If any child sees another child being maneuvered out of a playground or off a trail by a stranger, he or she should report it at once to another adult. I can remember once when a group of children screamed so loudly that they brought the police in time to save one of their comrades who was being manhandled by such a maniac. It is a wise precaution to come and go to parks and playgrounds with another child, rather than alone. It is also wise never to leave a playground (or anywhere else, in fact) with a stranger who tries to entice you away from your group.

I don't wish to imply that the woods and the streets and the parks are full of sexual monsters lying in wait to grab you when you are least expecting it. Not at all. But there are enough of them about so that every child should know of their existence and know how to avoid unnecessary encounters with them.

Seduction of young children is also considered a form of sexual sickness. Often the seducer is a member of the child's own family or a respected adult friend of the family whom the parents wouldn't dream of suspecting. Sometimes he or she holds a trusted position that brings him (or her) close to children, such as teacher, youth leader, priest, nun, or minister. (The records show that all of these professions—and others besides—have had such "guilty" members in their ranks.) Generally the seduction is without physical harm to the child, but because there is nearly always a certain amount of adult pressure on the child to conform to the wishes of the seducer, and because it is always carried on in secrecy, usually with an explicit instruction to keep it a secret, the seduced child can be very traumatized indeed. Sometimes the child actually enjoys the physical part of the seduction as much as the adult involved, but the harm comes because he or she knows (since there was a command to keep it secret) that this action is labeled "bad." A guilt load is thus built that is sometimes too much to bear, and the rest of the child's personality suffers. Furthermore, many (if not most) children who are seduced do not enjoy the physical experience, yet submit because they have been made afraid not to. This, as anyone may guess, is a sad state of affairs.

The worst part, however, is when discovery occurs and adults put up a great hue and cry about the harm the child has suffered. This makes a child feel that he or she has indeed been very bad and also that he or she is irrevocably damaged. Of course this isn't true.

A child should tell his or her parents if he or she is experiencing such seduction at the hands of any adult, even if that adult is one of the parents. Such an adult needs psychologic help (not punitive treatment, unless, of course, the seduction was molestation, which is something else again).

If the parents won't believe the child, he or she had better ask to see a family therapist or arrange an appointment with the school psychologist. Usually these professionals have dealt with enough similar situations to know that children are not talking about something preposterous or patently made up. They will treat the communication with confidence and help the child handle the delicate problem.

If the child is living in a single-parent family and that single parent is the seducer, the same advice holds. The child should take it upon himself or herself to talk with a trained therapist outside the home. These are found in schools and social agencies that deal with family problems. Sometimes a member of the clergy can guide a child to a professional for help.

Another "sick" expression of sex, though it is usually simply a nuisance, is the act of the Peeping Tom. Such a fellow gets his sexual kicks by peering in people's windows at night to watch them dress and undress or engage in other personal acts. If he gets caught criminal charges are generally pressed against him, though he needs psychiatric help rather than imprisonment.

Then there is the exhibitionist. Almost all of you, both boys and girls, though mostly girls, will at one time or another encounter such a sick individual. He is the man who, without provocation, unzips his pants and waves his penis at you. This is the "flasher," generally harmless and more like a pathetic small boy begging for his mother to approve of his maleness. However, the experience scares most girls considerably (and boys too). The thing to do is simply pass him by as quickly as possible and report him at once to the nearest police officer or to some other trusted adult. Such persons need treatment. In general, they won't harm you otherwise.

Sometimes in packed buses or in crowds anywhere, there are men who delight in "goosing" any female whom they can sidle up behind. They push their hand or their penis up against her buttocks under the pretense of being pressed into this position by the multitude. This kind of deviant who gets his sexual kicks at a girl's expense (or sometimes a boy's) is called a *frotteur*. The thing to do is to move away if you possibly can. Or turn and face him, loudly saying, "Excuse me, sir, but I'll thank you to leave me alone." If that doesn't work, appeal to the first kindly looking adult near you. You don't have to put up with being "goosed."

11 Deviant Sex Phenomena

Transvestism is a form of deviation in which a man (or a woman) gets sexual kicks by dressing in the clothes of the opposite sex. A male transvestite may collect lacy silk underwear, satin bras, nylon stockings, and high-heeled shoes, along with female jewelry, makeup, and a wig. And he gets a thrill out of appearing "in drag" in public. Sometimes transvestites form clubs and give parties (sometimes called "drag balls") among themselves, in which each tries to outdo the others in the femininity (or masculinity) of attire. Such orgies harm no one, of course, as long as they are held in private. Serious problems sometimes occur, for instance, when a man, completely bedecked as a woman, is discovered entering a public toilet labeled "Women."

A transvestite is not a homosexual—though many people make the mistake of thinking that he is. Nor is the transvestite harmful to anyone else.

A transsexual is one who truly believes that he or she was born in the skin of the wrong sex. The conviction is so strong that he or she will take any steps to get operated on to remedy the situation (to whatever degree it can be surgically remedied). Psychiatrists have tried unsuccessfully to treat such individuals without surgery in the hope that they could be persuaded to enjoy themselves in the bodies they were born in—but to no avail. Their only happiness seems to come when they have achieved the surgical operation they demand.

When such a patient applies for treatment, he or she is exposed to psychotherapy first to determine whether or not the problem may yield. If not, hormones and further psychotherapeutic help are given for a year or so. Only then is he or she accepted for surgery. After surgery there is careful training in living as a bona fide member of the opposite sex.

Many such transsexuals then live happy, creative lives and often they marry. Of course a man who is "made into a woman" can never have babies, nor can a woman who is transformed into a man produce sperm, but they can have the external look and feel of the sex they want to be, and they can live their lives as members of that sex.

It is hard and very expensive to obtain these operations, so it is lucky that this deviation is as rare as it is. The gender identity clinics that are emerging in large cities are of great help in providing information, and guidance, to those who suffer from transsexualism.

Sometimes brothers and sisters and other members of a close family group who share sleeping quarters with each other are enticed into having a variety of sexual experiences with each other. These generally come under the heading of "incest," which is against both our social mores and our legal code. Its effect on any individual child can be anything from profoundly harmful to mildly pleasant, depending on whether force and guilt or innocent play was involved. Many a brother and sister, or a pair of cousins, have experimented sexually and no harm has come of it. But just let a moralizing and scandalized adult catch them and give them hell for it, and the effect may be that one or both may carry a burden of deep shame for the rest of their lives.

There was a time in ancient Egypt when a pharaoh married his sister because she was the only one considered of royal enough blood to beget children of completely noble heritage. However, now marriage is forbidden between brothers and sisters, since their offspring will inherit in double portion the bad parts and the good parts of each. As you can see, this could either be disastrous, on the one hand, or lead to genius on the other, and is generally too risky for society to sanction. This law, however, has not prevented a lot of boys and girls from experimenting just the same.

Sometimes men associate an object with sexual arousal. For example, a small boy may have experienced his first awareness of sexual pleasure at a time when he was lying on the floor looking up at his mother. What he may have seen as he lay there was her pink underpants. Later he discovers that if he can look at a pair of pink underpants, he can get an erection. Later still, he may feel that he *has* to have this object in sight when he makes love. Such a compulsion is called fetishistic and the object is called a fetish.

Some people call fetishistic behavior "sick." However, it is harmful to no one and, at worst, may be only a nuisance to the man and his partner. Like all learned behavior, it is amenable to new conditioning, and as his experience in lovemaking grows he can learn to enlarge the range of stimuli that can affect his sexual responses. As you must have suspected by now, deviations from so-called normal sexual behavior, such as transvestism, fetishism, and transsexualism are not at all in the same class as those harmful acts that force sex upon an unwilling victim.

When you happen to observe them, it may be best if you refrain from judgmental reactions and, instead, try to understand how such behavior occurs.

12 Birth Control

Intercourse Without Making Babies

Ever since men and women first became aware of the relationship of sexual intercourse to the birth of babies, the problem of how to enjoy the one without risking the other has piqued their minds. It has also been deeply troubling that venereal disease has so frequently cast its shadow over the blissful enjoyment of sex. Let us now consider both of these important areas of responsibility.

Birth Control

Sex has the two marvelous functions of guaranteeing the continuance of the race and of drawing two people together in the deepest form of communion possible, making them feel at one with each other. Yet the question humankind has tried and is still trying to answer is how to have the unifying experience without having babies that can't be cared for. The problem of world overpopulation did not seem acute until the last century, because there were so many uncontrolled diseases which killed off people at very young ages, and thus the number of births didn't seem to matter—in fact, the more the better. Now, however, with the killing diseases largely conquered and the standard of living raised, year by year we have to face the problem of preventing the birth of babies unless we are ready to care for them.

If you have read about the population explosion, you

can truly believe that this is one of the most crucial issues of our day.

Fortunately for all of us, scientists have been at work devising better and better means of controlling birth, so that people can have babies only when and if they want them. To the individual family this can mean the difference between a life of sexual frustration and a life of sexual fulfillment.

Different methods of birth control work in different ways, but all depend on the motivation of the user to understand and follow instructions exactly. There is no such thing as grade C+ in Contraception. All grades must be A+ or the user is simply playing Russian roulette with his or her own life, as well as with that of another.

The Pill

The most effective method is the pill, which is used by women. It is manufactured by a number of drug companies under various trade names and is available by prescription from a doctor. A woman takes the pill every day, usually for twenty-one days. Then she stops and in a few days she starts menstruating. Five days from the start of menstruation, she once more starts taking the pills, and so the cycle continues. Some women do better on one kind of pill than another. This is even true among the various brands, due to different synthetics used. In any event, a woman should always be under the supervision of a physician when she starts using the pill, so that the type and strength of prescription can be regulated according to her individual reactions. Never trade pills with a friend. Her dosage may differ from yours. The same advice, incidentally, applies to any birth control device or medication that is specifically prescribed for you. There can be side effects for those using the pill. Some women find that it decreases their sexual desire. It can also cause temporary weight gain, and a few women may suffer hair loss, mood change, and even very dangerous blood clots. Low-dose mini-pills have fewer side effects but offer less safety from unwanted pregnancy.

The I.U.D.

A second reliable form of birth control (at least for those who can use it) is the Intra-Uterine Device—commonly known as the I.U.D. It is a small plastic- or copper-coated object made in various shapes and inserted into the uterus of the woman by a physician, or other specially trained technician. It remains in the uterus until the woman decides she wants to have a baby, at which time it is removed, again by a physician. Some of the new I.U.D.s release tiny quantities of hormone continuously for one year. These must be replaced once each year. Insertion of the I.U.D. can cause excessive cramping; there are also women whose uteruses are so active that they eject the device, and there are still others in whom it causes what is called "breakthrough" bleeding or even hemorrhaging. All this may just be too much to cope with for many women. However, for anyone who is able to use them at all, they are an excellent form of contraception, especially for someone who finds it hard to make decisions each time she makes love. Once an I.U.D. is inserted, she never has to think of it again until she has it changed or removed, except, of course, to check before intercourse that it is still in place by touching the plastic cord that hangs through the cervical opening and into the vagina.

The Diaphragm

A third form of birth control is the diaphragm (also used by the woman). It is time-tested and highly effective. It too has to be fitted by a doctor, and a woman must be taught to use it with precision. It is simply a flat, flexible rubber disc, the diameter of which is exactly measured so that the whole device fits over the cervix and thus prevents sperm from entering the uterus. A woman spreads a spermicidal jelly across its surface, and this serves both to lubricate the diaphragm (thus making it easier to insert) and to kill off sperm which come in contact with it during intercourse. She inserts it at any time (up to two hours) before lovemaking begins, and must leave it inside her for from six to eight hours after intercourse, at which time she may remove it. For each act of intercourse separated by several hours, she must add more cream or jelly.

When used correctly with the cream or jelly, the diaphragm is a very nearly perfect form of birth control. Some women and men, however, object to it because they say it is unromantic to have to bother with a mechanical procedure at a time when sexual love is at its peak. The answer, of course, is to take care of the insertion long before lovemaking begins. If this is done regularly as part of normal nighttime hygiene, like teeth-cleaning, it will no longer seem a mechanical interference. No woman would dream, for example, of running to the bathroom to clean her teeth just before she wanted to kiss a man she loved. She would have attended to such hygienic matters long before her lover arrived on the scene.

On the other hand, inserting the diaphragm can be incorporated into the lovemaking ritual. One additional advantage to a diaphragm is its possible use during menstruation as a temporary shield to keep excessive blood flow from interfering with sexual pleasure.

Sterilization

A permanent and usually irreversible form of birth control is sterilization, which probably none of you at your age should even consider. However, you should know of its existence.

Sterilization of the man consists of removing a small piece of each of the two vas deferens (tubes that carry sperm from the testes to the penis) and then tying off the ends. It is performed in the doctor's office under local anesthetics. Intercourse can then go on as before, but there are no sperm in the ejaculate. This method is usually undertaken only by men who have had all the children they want, who don't want children at all, or who, for medical reasons, should not have children.

Sterilization of the woman involves cutting and tying off the woman's Fallopian tubes so that egg and sperm can't meet. This is usually done in a hospital under anesthetic.

Foams and Condoms

Thus far, all the methods of birth control I have mentioned require the assistance of a physician along with careful instruction and practice in use under supervision. There are other methods that require neither prescriptions nor a physician's aid. However, they must be used with the same careful attention to detail if they are to be effective.

First are the contraceptive foams, such as Delfen or Emko which can be bought at any drugstore. (Don't confuse this with a vaginal douche.) These are used by the woman according to the instructions on the package. When inserted into the vagina the foam forms a spermicidal plug, coating the entrance to the cervix and thus not only prevents the entrance of the sperm but kills off sperm on contact.

Often, in conjunction with the woman's use of foam, a man can use a condom to raise the level of effectiveness of the foam. This combination, by the way, is close to a perfectly safe form of birth control when used conscientiously and with skill.

The condom is a sheath made of rubber or other flexible and liquid-proof material worn by the man. It must be carefully placed over his penis before it enters the vagina of the woman. He does this by rolling the condom over his erect penis, leaving a space at the tip for sperm to collect. After his ejaculation he must be especially careful to hold the upper edges of the condom so that it does not slip off as he withdraws his flaccid penis. A new condom should be used each time intercourse takes place.

Some men and women don't like a condom, claiming that it cuts down sensation slightly for both partners. However, this mild disadvantage is small indeed compared to the risk of having an unwanted child.

The condom is also highly effective in controlling the spread of infectious diseases like gonorrhea, syphilis, and fungus infections. I'll talk more about them in the next chapter.

Many young men and women wonder whose responsibility it is to provide birth control, the man's or the woman's. Actually, it is their mutual responsibility and anyone, male or female, starting intercourse without checking with each other on the adequacy of their birth control technique is asking for trouble.

To review, then, if absolute protection is desired, the pill is probably the best answer, though the potential side effects bear thoughtful consideration. A combination of the condom (used by the man) and either a foam or a diaphragm (used by the woman) would also provide close to perfect protection. Foam alone, diaphragm alone, or condom alone also provide high degrees of protection, but are not perfect.

I haven't even mentioned the Rhythm Method, because it is so unreliable; it is hardly feasible for those not prepared to have children should it fail, which it often does. It is based on the principle that a woman can get pregnant only during the time an ovum is descending the Fallopian tube, which occurs only once a month and takes only eight to twelve hours. This time of ovulation can be roughly determined by the woman if she takes her temperature the first thing every morning for a period of several months and keeps a record of these temperature readings. She then makes a graph with the days of the month forming one side of the graph and the readings the other. The graph will show a downward curve (of temperature) during the first part of the month, and then just at ovulation it will go up. The exact moment of ovulation will vary slightly from month to month. When she has kept a twelve-month record, she can note the variation in the timing of her ovulation dates. Thereafter she can abstain from intercourse each month during the period represented by the shortest to the longest interval at which ovulation took place, plus a day on each end to allow for the normal life of the sperm.

The trouble with the Rhythm Method, which is really just "timed abstinence," is that many factors can throw the rhythm off balance, such as an illness or emotional disturbance, or even a change in geographical location. Besides, many teenagers do not have regular periods.

It is more effective in helping people who *want* babies to pinpoint the times they *should* have intercourse than it is in helping those who don't want them.

There is still another form of controlling birth, which should be thought of, however, only as an emergency measure, like locking the barn door after the horse has been stolen. It is called the "Morning-After Pill." It is effective only if a woman under the care of a physician takes it within 3 days of an unprotected intercourse. (It takes approximately 3 days for a fertilized egg to descend the Fallopian tube and become implanted in the uterus.) The first dosage of The Morning-After Pill is often given as an injection. This medication seems to act by preventing implantation from occurring. It is put up in various dosages and in various forms, and must always be given under a doctor's supervision. It is, however, no picnic for a woman, as it often makes her temporarily sick. Also, if it does not bring on her period, it is imperative that she then have an abortion, since the hormones in the pill can damage the unborn child.

Many people have the incorrect notion that if a man withdraws his penis before ejaculation occurs (called the "Withdrawal Method"), a woman will not get pregnant. This is not so. Often there is a leakage of sperm prior to ejaculation, of which neither partner may be aware.

I have also mentioned earlier that even petting to orgasm has to be managed in such a way that no sperm are ejaculated near the entrance to the woman's vagina.

Many young people wonder how an unmarried person can obtain adequate help with birth control instruction. In fact, the very difficulty of getting adequate instruction and materials is one of the reasons which also make it advisable to use petting techniques for coming to orgasm, rather than intercourse, until one is a little older and can act with more responsible independence. There are some doctors, however, and a number of family planning clinics, who will advise the young on birth control methods such as the pill, the diaphragm, or the I.U.D. And there are, as I have noted, methods and materials that can be acquired without adult help.

If you are absolutely determined to have intercourse and cannot see the advantages of the noncoital route to sexual fulfillment, by all means give yourselves the benefit of all the safety you can provide. Better yet, go to a family planning clinic or to a youth service organization that will give you competent birth control advice and supervision, and is able to answer your questions confidentially in a straight way.

13 ⑤ Venereal Disease

What It Is, and
What to Do About It

Many books on sex for young people dwell at length on the horrors of venereal disease. I have not, and I don't intend to. However, it is important that you understand that they do exist, and they are nothing to laugh off as inconsequential, for indeed they can be horrendous. Furthermore, if every single human being accepted personal responsibility, the whole tragic matter of venereal disease could end in no time.

The word *venereal* stems from Venus, the goddess of love, and from the noun *venery*, meaning sexual intercourse. Venereal disease is contracted during intercourse from a partner who has it. Often the person who has the infection does not even know that he or she does have it, though usually it is at least suspected.

The two most commonly known forms are gonorrhea and syphilis, of which syphilis is much more serious. Gonorrhea starts as a local infection which attacks the genital organs of the female and the urinary tract of the male. The first symptoms turn up three to seven days after intercourse. In the male the symptoms consist of a burning sensation during urination, which is shortly followed by a puslike discharge from the urethra. In the female the symptoms may be painful urination followed by a vaginal discharge. Some women have no symptoms sufficiently disturbing to bother them, but they can be infected just the same. Penicillin is the drug used to cure gonorrhea, and it is very important that both partners be treated simultaneously so that they don't reinfect each other or infect other persons.

In recent years a new strain of gonorrhea which is resistant to penicillin has developed. Physicians and health departments are deeply disturbed about this, and several large-scale research studies have been launched to try to bring it under control.

Syphilis is caused by a small spiral-shaped bacteria called a spirochete. It is transmitted during intercourse or other intimate contact.

Once these bacteria have entered the body, the disease goes through four stages. In its early stage it causes a sore to appear at the part of the body where the germs enter, usually the genitals. This is called the primary stage. Shortly after, the secondary stage begins, which is usually ushered in by a generalized rash, along with small infectious ulcers of the mouth.

About then an infected person may develop syphilitic meningitis or some other form of syphilis of the nervous system. Eventually the disease goes into a latent period and may be dormant for years, only to reappear in such diseases as paresis (a form of insanity, commonly called softening of the brain), severe heart disease, or blindness or locomotor disability.

Detection of syphilis can be made through a blood test. This test, by the way, is required for a marriage certificate in most states. Young couples who have intercourse before marriage should be prepared to offer each other a clean bill of health, as determined by such a blood test, before having intercourse. Alternatively, they should know positively that they have never had sexual contact with an infected person.

The treatment for syphilis is penicillin or a substitute (for those who are allergic to penicillin). It is important to have at least two follow-up blood tests as checks to be sure treatment has been complete.

Syphilis can be successfully cured in 99 percent of cases if it is treated at the stage before the rash begins. If the rash has emerged the success rate then drops slightly, but not significantly. In the latent period the serious consequences can also be almost completely avoided by treatment. In other words, if people who suspect that they may have contracted syphilis would go to a doctor or a venereal disease clinic promptly, they would have very little to fear.

The increase in syphilis in persons under twenty years of age in the past decade is horrendous. The statistics, of course, include large numbers of promiscuous and grossly careless individuals. While the increase is something to make any serious young person think long and soberly, it is not mentioned here to frighten those of you who are seriously in love and who have an intelligent respect for your own bodies and the bodies of those you love. It is, however, additional evidence pointing to the fact that good sexuality depends upon your ability to be utterly trustworthy and to keep your body in a healthy state.

In all my years of practice as a marriage counselor, I have encountered only a handful of persons who have contracted a venereal disease. What this means is that where a man or woman is highly selective about the person with whom he or she makes love, and where the partners limit their lovemaking to each other, there is very little chance of contracting venereal disease.

What has concerned me much more than venereal disease has been the high incidence of other forms of vaginal infections which are very annoying and which do interfere with pleasurable sexuality. Little is ever mentioned about them, and yet their presence can temporarily ruin a woman's chance for sexual pleasure in intercourse and cause her to become very irritated and irritable besides.

The two most common of these infections are monilia and trichomoniasis.

Monilia is a fungus infection and causes a whitish discharge. It often stings and burns, and the vaginal tissues may become so irritated from the discharge that intercourse is painful. It should be treated by a physician. Many doctors pay altogether too little attention to the necessarily prolonged treatment of monilia. They also pay too little attention to treating the sexual partner of a girl who is suffering from it. While men don't suffer from these infections, they can carry them and reinfect the girl after she has been successfully treated. Then the whole process begins again.

It is difficult to determine the incidence of monilia, but a great many women report a history of having had it at one time or another. If a woman feels itchy, burning sensations in her vagina, she should at once seek help from her gynecologist and should not be content with temporary cessation of symptoms. She should insist on being checked at intervals for at least three months to see that the medication she has been given has completely eradicated any evidence of monilia.

Trichomoniasis is another bothersome infection. It causes a foamy, offensive-smelling discharge which is produced by the trichomonas parasite. There is an oral antitrichomonal drug which your doctor can prescribe, and treatment should be instituted at once as this condition is highly infectious and very irritating. The discharge causes a burning sensation, chafing of the skin in the vulvar region, and itching.

In general, if there is any vaginal discomfort or discharge, a woman should check with her gynecologist. I might say that these infections carry no sociosexual implications as do the venereal diseases, for they are acquired in many ways and are not necessarily associated with sexual intercourse. However, their negative effect on the pleasure of sexual intercourse is profound.

14 Birth of a Baby
Wanted and Unwanted

Physically, a human baby enters this world very much like other mammals. Though we deal with this in detail in Chapter 16, let's take a moment here to review the basic facts.

A male impregnates a female by inserting his penis into her vagina; then, by a series of in-and-out movements, he stimulates the ejaculation of his seminal fluid, which contains sperm that have been manufactured in his testicles. (Each teaspoon of seminal fluid contains millions of sperm.) These merge with liquid secreted by the female's vaginal lining and immediately start a swimming spree, wiggling their way up through her cervix into her uterus and on into her Fallopian tubes. There, if an egg (called ovum) happens to be descending, one of the sperm may join with it. The merging of sperm and egg is called fertilization. (If two or more sperm manage to enter an egg, twins or triplets are formed.) The fertilized egg descends to the woman's uterus, where it becomes implanted in the lining, sucking up nourishment much as a plant sucks up life from the soil. There it grows at a phenomenal rate for the next nine months; then, through a process of muscular contractions called labor, it is pushed out through her vagina, emerging as a human baby. At the time of its birth it may weigh about seven pounds and be approximately nineteen to twenty inches long.

These biological facts, however, don't begin to tell of

the drama and excitement of any person's conception and birth.

Ask your mother to tell you about your own birth. Ask her what led her to decide to have you. How long did it take her before she became pregnant? How did she feel about it when she knew that you were actually on the way? How did your father react when she told him? Did they hope for a boy or a girl? Did she find it hard or easy to carry a baby inside her? When did she first feel you kicking? Were you a very active baby or a peaceful, quiet one as you were growing? Did she go to a hospital to have you? Was your father with her? Was he permitted to watch you being born? Did you come out head first (most babies do), feet first (called breech birth), or by Caesarean section (a surgical procedure in which the mother's abdomen is cut open and the baby extracted by the doctor)? This is done when the cervix does not dilate or when the mother's vaginal opening is too small to let the baby pass through. Of course, the operation is done under anesthesia and in an operating room. How long was your mother in labor? Did you cry right away or did you have to be helped to breathe? And how did your mother feel about you? Glad? Tired? Disappointed in your sex? Glad about your sex? Did she nurse you and, if so, did she enjoy it? (Nursing is a wonderful sensation for the mother, as well as for the baby. It is, in fact, sexually pleasurable to her, though some mothers are afraid to admit this.)

Try to get your mother talking about your birth. You'll learn a lot. Birth is something no mother ever forgets. Besides, it's a story she owes to you, so that you can have a deeper appreciation of the preciousness of your life.

There is a vast difference, of course, in how mothers feel about their pregnancies, depending in large measure on whether they are ready, willing, and eager to start a family, or have accidentally become pregnant. To those who have wanted and planned for their babies, pregnancy is welcomed with great joy as a marvelous fulfillment of a life dream. To those who don't want a baby, pregnancy is an interruption of life and often leaves a woman feeling like someone who has been pushed off a high diving board when she hasn't yet learned to swim.

Until recently, when a woman married, she knew that she was gambling on the probability of pregnancy, sooner or later. And the unmarried woman who indulged in sexual intercourse took the same gamble. But today any woman, married or unmarried, can have sexual intercourse without that gamble. She can choose whether she will or will not have a child. Some women, however, do not exercise that choice. They still gamble, and sometimes the stakes are tragically high.

Let's imagine, now, two different kinds of pregnancies—one unwanted and the other wanted.

Judith and John will illustrate the first. They are not only real persons, but their experience is like that of thousands of other teenagers who struggle with an unwanted pregnancy.

Judith was just sixteen when she and John experimented sexually a little farther than either of them had intended. They had been "so sure" that they could "get by" just this once, and that, if they enjoyed the experience, they'd go to a birth control clinic and get some "protection" for future times.

As you have guessed, Judith got pregnant and then was so scared about it that she made a bad mistake in judgment. She didn't tell her parents until it was far too late for her to have an abortion.

Let me digress a moment here, for some of you may not know what that word means. An abortion is a way of terminating a pregnancy before a baby has developed sufficiently to survive outside its mother. This is usually done within the first three months of pregnancy, during which time it is a relatively simple surgical procedure (done under local analgesia and in a medical setting). At one time abortion was illegal, but this is no longer true, and any female who chooses not to have a baby, for good and sufficient reasons of her own, may apply to her doctor or to a clinic set up for this purpose and may have her pregnancy terminated. However, it is not a decision to enter into lightly. And certainly it is not a substitute for good birth control. Actually, it is a method of last resort, for use in situations like Judy's or when, in spite of care, a birth control method has failed. But it *is* a solution to unwanted pregnancy. After three months, however, few doctors feel comfortable about performing an abortion, since the risks become much greater and many religious groups consider that an embryo has by then become "a person." Some even claim that it is murder to remove it, though this does seem a bit farfetched if you consider that no embryo could live at that stage outside its mother.

Let's go back to Judy. She had passed up her chance for a legal abortion by not discussing the matter of her pregnancy with anyone who could be of real help. Her wisest solution, of course, would have been to terminate her pregnancy. But by five months, when the baby had begun to move, and she had begun to look very pregnant, it was altogether too late. And of course by that time her parents, John, and John's parents were all involved.

Let me emphasize again what a pity it was that she didn't confide in her own parents the moment she suspected pregnancy. No matter what she might have *thought* their reaction would be, no matter how much hurt or anger or shame she expected from them, in the end she would have found that they would have stood by her. Many young men and women say, "It would kill my parents to know," and then they, like Judy, try to solve their problem alone. Only when they discover that this is not a problem that can be solved without adult help do they confide in their parents, as was the case with Judy. If you (or a friend) should ever find yourself in such a situation, by all means go to your parents at once and frankly tell them that your impulsive love has led you to go beyond what you had intended. Admit that you have made a serious mistake in judgment and that you need their help in making a decision as to what to do next. Sometimes both the boy's parents and your parents will want to confer with you. But sometimes there is such estrangement between families when an unwanted pregnancy occurs that this is not possible. Some angry words fly that are later bitterly regretted. But in the long run, parents do calm down: they don't die of grief or shame and most have weathered enough other kinds of emergencies to have developed very good problem-solving techniques which you can (and will) benefit from. Their impulse, like yours, may be to go cry on the shoulders of their best friends. I hope that neither you nor they (if you are ever in such a spot) will indulge in such nonsense. The first principle, when in personal trouble, is to discuss your private affairs with someone who is equipped by training and motivation to help you. Actually, there are only four major decisions to choose from in a situation such as Judy's.

The first, and best, namely, termination of her pregnancy, had already been made impossible by her silence.

The second, marriage: she could marry John and they could try their best to make a go of a difficult situation. However, the chance of their being able to support themselves was almost zero. Furthermore, the education both wanted and needed would be severely curtailed, and even under conditions of help from parents they would still be dependents, still children. Try as they might to pretend that they would be running their own show, they would not be.

And this would irk them, just as dependence irks anyone who wants to be in control of his or her own life.

Another factor involved in an early marriage is of even greater significance, namely, the baffling matter of personality change that goes on between the ages of fifteen and twenty-two or twenty-three. The person you love and admire at seventeen may not be at all the one you want to spend the rest of your life with at twenty-two. This is not always the case, but it happens often enough to make most twenty-two-year-olds shudder when they imagine marriage with some of the persons they were infatuated with at seventeen.

However, in some individual instances, and perhaps John's and Judy's had a chance of being one of these, where both are highly motivated to make the marriage work, despite handicaps, where they can get some needed support from parents or other adults, and where they love each other, they might find that marrying could be the best choice for them.

Third choice was for Judy to have the baby and give it up for adoption. This would be a very hard choice, but maybe a good one. She could go to a social agency or to her own doctor and she would be directed and counseled all along the way. Depending on her financial needs, she might or might not be given financial help with medical bills. Sometimes prospective adoptive parents are only too happy to underwrite these, though most states do not permit adoptive parents to pay more of a pregnant woman's expenses than her medical ones. Some women think that they can never gather the courage to give up their baby for adoption, but most, after months of sober thought and counseling, find that this answer is often best for the baby and best for themselves. Particularly if she is still a girl and not yet a woman, her own life then has a chance to develop to maturity before taking on the burdens of maturity, and she has the deep comfort of knowing that she has given the precious gift of newborn life to a loving couple who have longed for a child yet could not have one of their own.

The fourth choice for Judy was to have the baby and keep it, raising it herself, without marrying John. Only a highly motivated, strong, and competent person can do this successfully. Furthermore, she would have to use much ingenuity to locate resources to help her. Like the mother who plans to give up her baby for adoption, she could utilize the services of social agencies. Many would help her find jobs where she could render some service and still look after her own baby. Perhaps, best of all, her own parents would help her. She might be able to live at home and in one way or another continue her education as soon as her child was big enough to attend a child-care center. Perhaps her mother would care for her child while she finished her education—but this is supposing a lot. Most forty-year-old grandmothers these days have jobs of their own or feel that they have done their stint with child care.

Make no mistake about it, caring for a baby alone is a demanding and lonely task. It is certainly any woman's right to make that choice, but it is not a bed of roses. A girl should think long and carefully before committing herself to this choice.

In the instance of John and Judy, their decision was for marriage since they cared a great deal for each other and because both sets of parents agreed to help them financially until John could finish high school and get a job. They were lucky in having parents who could and would help, but just the same it was quite a blow to have to give up their dream of college, since there just wasn't enough money for them to have both college and a baby.

After a wedding in the county courthouse (not at all the

kind that Judith had anticipated for herself), they moved into two rooms on the top floor of Judy's family home, and there tried to set up housekeeping of sorts, though in fact they were but teenage members of Judith's own family.

Judith experienced the movements of the baby as an uncomfortable reminder of her changed life. For a long time she resisted recognition of the sensation at all; in fact she had concentrated her entire attention on her life above her waistline, and had indulged herself in a kind of fantasy that what was happening below it was simply not happening to her. When it was no longer possible to ignore it, she reacted to the baby's movements by tightening her abdomen. This, of course, did not give the developing baby as much freedom to move as it might have had if she could have relaxed and enjoyed those movements.

Judith's mother urged her to prepare a few things for the baby's reception, which she did—perfunctorily. John tried to be a comfort, but his real interests lay in his life at school and with their other friends, from whom he felt somewhat cut off. Besides, he was worried and very distressed at having to forgo college when his friends were all talking and planning their future education. But he was not nearly as cut off as Judy was. John at least had school, but Judith had to remain at home after her pregnancy became apparent. Her school system would not allow a pregnant girl to continue in regular high school classes. She did go to some continuation school classes for adults, but it was not the same.

She also went to a maternity center where expectant mothers could learn about giving birth and about the care of babies. But she felt out of place in the midst of happy mothers bursting with enthusiasm for their "coming events." After attending twice, she dropped the class. And she told her doctor that she didn't want to have anything to do with "this natural childbirth business." And, she added,

"I want to be as little conscious during labor and delivery as it is safe for me to be, and I don't want to nurse the baby!"

The doctor was a kindly woman who realized Judy's distress about her premature leap into motherhood, and she offered to permit John to be with Judy during labor, thinking it might be a comfort to her. But Judy said she'd rather just have her mother with her.

When it came time for Judy's delivery, she and her mother went off to the hospital, while her father and John tried to keep uneasy company at home, and later in the hospital waiting room.

Judith put up with the indignity of being shaved, given an enema, and then, to her consternation, being left alone. (Her mother was banished to the waiting room, since no one had had the presence of mind to encourage her presence at her daughter's side, and her mother had not known enough to protest. In her day, it was the regular procedure to banish all family members to waiting rooms.)

Time ticked away. The doctor came and went, giving Judy what encouragement she could. Judy was in hard labor, but her cervix somehow did not open up. More hours. She wanted John with her, but when she asked for him and he came, he soon showed that he didn't know how to give her the help and comfort she needed; so, in the end, she sent him away again. At last her labor had results and she was taken to the delivery room where she was finally anesthetized, and the baby was taken from her by high-forceps delivery. (This means that the doctor had to assist her body to push the baby out, by fitting surgical instruments around the baby's head and thus extracting the baby through the vaginal opening.)

When she awakened from the anesthesia, the doctor asked if she would like to hold her fine baby boy, but Judy was too sleepy, too drugged, and also uninterested. All she really wanted just then was to drop back into blessed sleep and to experience her own body as once more belonging to just herself alone.

Later, when a nurse brought the baby in to be breast-fed, she again stated that she did not intend to nurse. However, she did take her son into her arms and really looked at him for the first time. The more she looked the more connected she felt, and it was then that she began to have a sense of love, pride, and achievement. "I am somebody's mother," she murmured over and over to herself as if for reassurance.

A few days later Judith left the hospital, glad to be out, but it was then that her problems really began. John, at seventeen, tried his best to be a father and a comforting husband, but the fact is that his heart just wasn't in it, and he soon found that he had no taste for the nitty-gritty of baby care. He began to appreciate the statistic that one in two teenage marriages ends in divorce. Heretofore he had thought that statistics were a bore—that they applied to somebody else. But a baby crying in the night—demanding that he, John, walk him and sing to him and bottle him and change his diaper—was just not his cup of tea. He began to look forward to the end of high school so that he could hunt a job that would occupy his whole day, instead of having to turn up at home the moment school was over to relieve Judy for other chores.

Little by little, Judith, out of necessity, developed the skills to care for her baby, though she often ran downstairs to her own mother in a panic when the baby howled with colic, which he often did during those first six weeks of life.

But while Judith gradually became a "mother," since life demanded this of her, John eventually opted out of being a father. Their high school romance had long since lost its appeal, and after a while he moved back in with his own parents, acknowledging to Judith and to society, and to himself, that he simply did not have what it takes to go on with marriage and parenthood. He promised to do what he could to help out financially, but, as for partnership with a woman and fatherhood, he was not ready.

Let's consider now another kind of birth—a *wanted* one. You can pretend that it is your own—whether it is your story or not.

Go deep down into your fantasy world. Let your mind's eye see a tiny ovum just beginning its descent from your mother's ovary. In a few seconds it will make contact with a sperm from your father's body. Your mother and father have anticipated this moment with their whole beings. They have lived together for several years, they have created a strong and wonderful union with each other and they are both engaged in work that they enjoy and have prepared themselves to do. But for some months past, they have felt a deep longing to add to their family and to share their love with a baby. It is in this moment of time that you are created.

Imagine, now, that several months have passed and that you are beginning to move about in your mother's womb. Try some gentle exploratory movements here and now and see what they feel like. You are in a dark warm cave and yet you are not troubled by the dark. You are busy learning to move and you are growing at the fastest rate that you will ever grow again in your whole life. You double and redouble and redouble again in size. And you find it a fantastic experience.

Some very nice things happen to you sometimes—like when your mother stretches out her whole languorous body in a warm tub of water and, lying there, taps her tummy in a kind of telegraphic message to you that seems to say, "I love you, I love you." You want to answer back, so when she taps, you kick—and a wonderful game is in progress. You, *inside*, feel connected with something *outside* that *wants* connection with you.

In the meantime, you are still continuing to grow bigger and bigger. And you hear sounds. Your movements are stronger and stronger, and then comes a day when you find your warm little cave very cramped indeed. To your surprise you also find yourself descending into the very pit of the cave and you feel your head being used as a kind of wedge, while powerful forces, not under your control, press you farther and yet farther into a very tight passage. You are frightened and you can't move and there is nothing you can do but allow yourself to be catapulted onward. All of a sudden the pressure stops and you are in the hands of something, someone, that conveys to you a sense of warmth and reassurance. You let out a gasp as you draw your first breath. Then you are placed in your mother's reaching arms and, snuggling there, you hear her say, "My darling baby, my darling baby, welcome to this earth!" as she licks the top of your fuzzy head with her tongue in a welcoming caress.

The kind, firm hand takes you again and cuts the cord that has attached you to your mother. Then you are laid once more on her tummy. Your father is there too. His face is alight with smiles. Two pairs of eyes now warm you through and through with their overwhelming joy in your arrival.

Presently all three of you are in a bedroom and you are curled up between your mother and daddy. You are being offered your mother's breast to suck. This is the most delicious and wonderfully satisfying experience that you have known so far. You decide right then and there that if this is what life outside your cave is like, you'll stick around awhile and sample more of it. You suck long and hard, as if the impulse came from the very depths of your being. Your whole world is centered in your mother's breast. Then something else occurs. Your pleasure is so intense that you suddenly find your whole body aquiver—a forerunner of that wonderful quiver that you will later come to know and enjoy as orgasm.

You hear your mother and father talking about the satisfaction of taking care of you. They tell each other in your hearing that you've come along at just the right moment in their lives for them to enjoy you most. You look around and see the loving care that has gone into preparation for your arrival: a cosy room, bright with sunlight and color, a soft blanket that your tiny fingers curl around and sometimes your mouth sucks, a crib that allows you to see your surroundings. You like it best when your mother and your father put you between them on the bed and you feel the warmth of their love radiating back and forth between them, providing invigorating nourishment to you. Sometimes your father carries you about in his strong arms singing ribald ditties to you which you are crazy about. You immediately settle down in his arms and drop off to dreamland. Soon you discover that there is a long period each day when your father is not home, but you sense his eager excitement as he approaches you each night, as if he could hardly wait to get there to give you your nightly bath. You are glad to be alive.

Now, in present time, slowly come back up to the here and now. Did you enjoy this birth? Do you like being the wanted child of loving, secure parents? Is this the kind of birth you are going to give your child?

You can, you know, unless you lose your head and your sense of judgment. To have a wanted and prepared-for baby is one of the most rewarding of all life's experiences. To have an unwanted one is one of its worst.

If you use birth control, restraint, or noncoital methods of lovemaking, you can usually have your baby when you want it and not when you don't. If you don't do any of these things, but just plunge ahead, you are playing Russian roulette.

You can be in charge of your life and not a victim. Having a baby is an active process and not something that "has to happen."

15 Sex Myths

Debunking the Scaremongers

There are very few subjects that have had as many myths and taboos attached to them as sex.

A famous psychiatrist, Wilhelm Reich, once pointed out that the most effective way for one person (or class) to control others is to make them afraid of their own sexuality, for a sexually positive person is likely to resist the power peddlers. History has shown that he was right. From the very earliest times conquerors tried, in one way or another, to emasculate those they wanted to dominate. It made slaves more tractable. And the "old men" of any tribe (ancient or modern) learned also that if they wanted to retain power and authority, if they wanted to be "boss of the show," as it were, all they had to do was set up a system of taboos about sex and they could minimize the superior physical strength and vitality of the young.

There have been other motivations for sexual taboos, of course, many springing from well-intentioned ignorance. For example, until very recently birth control was nonexistent. So if parents wanted to protect their girl children from premature pregnancy, they resorted to fear methods to subdue sexuality until adult status had been reached. It was certainly wise on the part of parents to try to forestall premature reproduction, but the "scare-ache" method has never led to mental health nor, in fact, to positive action, though it certainly was effective in permanently limiting the ability of millions of people to experience sexual fulfillment, even after they reached maturity.

Another motivation for myths is to provide a cover for sheer ignorance. If you don't know the "why" or the "how" of a phenomenon, you make up an explanation to allay your own anxiety (for nothing seems to make people more nervous than the unknown). Then, if the "explanation" (however inaccurate) is repeated often enough and long enough, it gains the strength of a tradition and people begin to believe it as a fact of life.

Do you remember the nursery story about Henny Penny who started a regular stampede of calamity when she cackled "The sky is falling" after she had been hit on the head by something which she didn't bother to identify?

Menstruation Myths

Sex taboos and myths grow up like that. A woman dies of pneumonia, let's say, and friends, casting about for an adequate reason, hit upon the coincidence that she had gone swimming while having her menstrual period. So they start putting two and two together and arriving at five. After a bit the myth becomes, "If you go swimming during your period, something dreadful will happen to you." After a while, it becomes even more distorted: "If you take a bath during your period, it is very bad for you."

Now today every educated person knows that of all times when a woman needs a bath, it is during her menstrual period. Most women know that they can swim, hike, dance, work, or do anything else they please during their menstrual periods as long as they don't overdo (which is also true in their nonmenstrual days).

A woman can also enjoy sex during her menstrual period. The taboo of no sex during menstruation is a very great deprivation for both men and women—yet, in spite of all scientific findings to the contrary, many people still cling to this silly taboo, maybe some of them because it serves as an excuse for not doing what they don't want to do anyway.

Menstrual blood itself has been invested with all kinds of magic power, ranging from the elixir of life to deadly poison. It is none of these things, of course. Rather it is the nourishment on which an embryonic baby would have survived had conception occurred. Someday, probably, an inventive person will figure out a way to make a nourishing skin cream out of menstrual waste—but in the meantime the myths go on and on.

Menstrual cramps are not a result of sexual activity—more likely the reverse. The old comment, meant to be a comfort to a girl, "Wait till you're married and you won't have cramps anymore," seemed to infer that marriage was what conferred the immunity from pain. Actually, many girls are relieved of cramps if they masturbate just at the start of their menstrual period. If this doesn't help, a girl should go to her doctor and get him (or her) to give her some analgesic medicine. Again, the myth that women are supposed to suffer (or, as some dim-witted psychoanalysts explain, "Women enjoy pain") is hogwash. No one enjoys pain and there is no reason for any girl to suffer.

It is a fact that some girls (and women) do get low and droopy the week before they menstruate, but these emotional low spots can often be alleviated by the administration of hormones. If you suffer deep depression that really bugs you, go see a good gynecologist (preferably a woman) who is sympathetic and knowledgeable about such things.

Some of the more absurd myths surrounding menstruation are these:

Milk turns sour if handled by a menstruating woman.

Only married women should use tampons. (You can guess why this one was invented: to keep young girls from discovering their own bodies and finding that these do, indeed, feel very good.)

A boy can tell if you're menstruating by looking in your eyes.

Menstruation has been called everything from "falling off the roof" to "the curse." It has held a position both sacred and shameful: symbol of potential fertility, yet, in its absence, symbol of sexual activity, which brands one as "bad."

Many sexual myths, particularly those concerned with menstruation, originate in individual families and become very ingrained. If mother has pain during menstruation and goes to bed for three days, so does daughter. It is what is expected and what is done, generation after generation.

More Masturbation Myths

Menstruation, of course, is only one aspect of sex that has collected taboos. Those associated with autoeroticism (masturbation) would fill a book. Furthermore, because every last child, male and female, discovers its genitals very early in life, and because the taboo against encouraging any sexual feeling until marriage has been so prevalent, all kinds of "no-nos" have cursed this otherwise fun time of self-gratification.

You'll go crazy.

You'll go blind.

If you masturbate now, you won't enjoy sex in marriage.

Your penis will drop off.

God will punish you.

Anyone can tell by looking at you whether you do that.

You'll get pimples if you do.

You'll infect yourself.

You'll weaken your brain.

You'll go to hell. Sex is only for those who are willing to take on the responsibility of having children.

It's all right to do it if you don't do it too much. (And then no one tells you how much is too much.)

The Catholic church made it a matter for confession (an occasion of mortal sin) at one time, though, in most parts of the civilized world today, this edict has been relaxed as priests have become more knowledgeable. Many Catholics, however, still feel a deep sense of guilt about masturbation. I have already written about autoeroticism and the fact that it is a good thing, not a bad thing. Obviously, all of the myths and taboos are false, so enjoy your self-pleasuring. It is God's own gift to you, especially while you are too young for other forms of sexuality.

Sexist Myths

There are a raft of myths that might be called "sexist myths." Some people still believe in some of them—but they are all false, and behavior that assumes their "accuracy" can be very damaging to relations between the sexes.

Here are some—and you will think of many more:

Boys are smarter than girls.

A girl is responsible for saying no because a boy never has enough control.

Men know more about sex than women.

Men like sex better than women.

A man needs it and a woman doesn't. (How about that!)

No man wants second-hand goods. (Another version is damaged goods.)

If you sleep with a man he'll never marry you.

A bride's virginity is her most precious dowry.

A man should have experience; a woman, innocence

(ignorance!). By the way, today men are more afraid of marrying a woman who is a virgin than of the reverse. Virginity, in the minds of today's young men, may mean frigidity.

Women are not supposed to enjoy sex.

A woman is a baby-making machine and loses her value as a human being if she is barren. (Today the world needs fewer babies, not more, and we don't hear so much about "barren" women.)

Little girls should keep their legs together or they are asking for sex.

A woman is a whore if she sleeps with a man before marriage. But a man is supposed to "try it out" with her before he leaps into marriage with her.

The Myth of the Wedding Night

The wedding night, of course, was good for all sorts of myths, some so fantastic as to be downright unbelievable. Some that still persist sound like these:

Just do anything that comes naturally—you don't have to have any special education for sex.

If you don't have a hymen, you're not a virgin.

If you don't bleed on your first intercourse (on your wedding night, of course), you don't have a hymen.

First intercourse is excruciating.

First intercourse is heavenly and something you can only have once, so save it for the man you love. (Incidentally, it generally takes *many* sessions of lovemaking and a lot of knowledge to reach that degree of skill that results in what could be called "heavenly.")

Penis Myths

Just as girls have suffered a lot of unnecessary agony

from menstruation myths, boys have suffered from what could be called "size, shape, and color myths"—such as the following (all of which are false):

A big penis is more virile. (Actually, it is the skill of use, not size, that spells virility.)
A longer penis means better lovemaking, and is more exciting to a woman.
A hairy man is more virile.
Black men make better lovers.
Big men are more exciting sexually.

"Tall, dark, and handsome" is the fairy tale prototypeof the "perfect" lover, just as "blonde, blue-eyed, and petite" is supposed to be every man's ideal princess. Neither is, of course, but plenty of teenagers have lost sleep over these myths.

V.D. Myths

V.D. (venereal disease) myths have scared a lot of people, especially teenagers (as they were meant to do by those who promulgated them). V.D. is, indeed, something to be scared about—but before one can act intelligently, one has to sort out truth from fiction.

Nonsense like the following should be discounted:

You can get V.D. from drinking cups.
Only loose and dirty people catch V.D.
If you let someone touch your vagina, you will get V.D.

The truth is that V.D. is no respecter of class, cleanliness, or morals. A girl may be virginal and yet pick up V.D. the very first time she sleeps with her infected partner, who may, indeed, come from a fine family, take baths regularly, and otherwise be a gentleman. Or she may have had a multitude of lovers, none infected, and never catch V.D. You have to be exposed to V.D. to get it.

A good practice for all lovers contemplating intercourse is to offer each other a clean bill of health. If there has been previous sexual experience with other partners about whom there may be some doubt, the bill of health would include a medical examination involving a blood test for syphilis and a culture test (women) or a quick gram stain test (men) for gonorrhea; also a test for the presence of trichomoniasis or monilia. It is as much a part of expressing love responsibly as offering a beloved partner a trustworthy character.

There are so many misunderstandings about the communicability of sexual infections that young people owe it to themselves to get clear on these. Trichomoniasis and monilia, for example, which most men think are only "women's diseases" that can't be carried or gotten by men, can indeed be both. Actually, trichomoniasis is very contagious, and a man can carry it from one woman to the next. He can even reinfect the original woman after she has been "cured." The only answer for a man who knows he has been with someone who has "trich" is to undergo treatment right along with her and to make sure that he is completely free of it before making love either to her or to anyone else. (Condoms help, in this respect, and many a man has prevented himself from becoming infected or from being a carrier by using them.)

Monilia (another fungus infection) loves to live in dark, damp places, and the vagina is a perfect site for it to take hold. Many people, even some physicians, have claimed that men don't get monilia and don't carry it—but this is not so. Monilia attacks the mucus membrane lining of the digestive tract as well as of the vagina. A man engaging in mouth-genital lovemaking with an infected woman may end up with moniliasis of his intestinal tract—and this is not very pleasant. So it is a myth that fungus infections are to be treated lightly or not treated at all. And it is equally a myth that every permissive girl is a carrier of syphilis or gonorrhea.

Infectious disease of any kind, whether of nose, throat, skin, or sex organ, needs to be treated medically and no one, married or unmarried, should "share" his or her infection along with his or her love.

Drugs and Fantasy

There are some myths relating to the effect of alcohol and drugs on sexuality that we've already touched on—but let me repeat the most common ones here:

A drink will help you feel sexier. Obviously untrue. It may loosen your inhibitions, but excessive drinking may also deprive you of your ability to get an erection if you are a boy or reduce your responsiveness if you are a girl.

Pot makes sex better. As far as science can discover, marijuana does not improve the erotic experience, though a few people report that the distortions they experience are useful for them.

In my long practice as a sex counselor, I have always taken a "sex history" of anyone asking for help. The history goes along swimmingly until I get to the question, "What about your sex fantasies?" Then there is a sudden silence and complete dearth of information on the part of many persons. I wonder if they feel that something is wrong with them if they indulge in sex fantasies. Of course there isn't. All people have sex fantasies unless they have been so repressed at so young an age that they just can't remember those they did have and don't dare produce any more.

Fantasies are a rich and pleasurable part of sexuality

and perfectly healthy. Furthermore, a fantasy does not represent at all what a person would actually do, or even want to do, in reality.

Fantasies have the effect of speeding up and intensifying sex excitement and sometimes it is the "taboo," rather than the "wished for" idea that performs this function. You know how tingly and excited you got when you were playing hide-and-seek and *almost* got caught. This doesn't mean that you *wanted* to get caught—but only that the "almost caught" feeling is sexually exciting. So it is with many a taboo fantasy.

Almost everyone has a favorite sex fantasy, sometimes a whole slew of them, and, people usually fantasize, even when they are making love with a partner they adore. The myth is, of course, that you never need to fantasize when you are making love with a real person, but this simply isn't true.

Another myth is that men fantasize but women don't. If you believe this you should read some of the recent popular books containing collections of women's sexual fantasies (such as Nancy Friday's *The Secret Garden*).

Orgasm Myths
Here are some myths about orgasm:

Mutual orgasm is the only good thing. Actually, mutual orgasm represents a peak sexual experience that skillful lovers who are in close harmony with each other's body rhythms sometimes enjoy. However, orgasm, whether before, after, or even without your partner, is very enjoyable indeed.

A man has to "make" a girl come. It's the man's responsibility to "bring" the woman. The truth is that unless a woman can "bring" herself, she has a poor chance of "coming" with any man. Orgasm is something that each partner is responsible for and something they share to-gether, as they would a wonderful dance requiring skill from both. No one would expect a dancer, for example, to create a fine ballet with a partner who had never practiced walking, let alone dancing. A man can be a willing and pa-tient teacher, and he can learn how a woman likes to be made love to, but he cannot "make" her "come." She has to do that for herself.

A very harmful orgasm myth, promoted by sexist psychoanalytic therapists (more's the pity—though they are now learning that they are wrong and are trying to change their tune), is that vaginal orgasm is the only truly mature form of orgasm and that a woman who arrives at orgasm by stimulating her clitoris is resorting to an imma-ture form of sexual pleasuring. All scientific research today has given the lie to this myth. It's as unreasonable for a woman *not* to stimulate her clitoris (which is the key to her sexual pleasure) as it would be for a man not to stimulate his penis in intercourse.

Another orgasm myth is that the quality of the orgasm is always the same. This is not true, of course, since orgasm relates intimately to a person's total emotional state at the time of the experience. Orgasm can come on as wildly as a tidal wave or as gently as the lapping at a ship's side in a calm sea.

Conception Myths

Along with orgasm myths there are conception myths galore. Here are a few:

"You only have to do it once to get pregnant." If you have read the rest of this book, you already know that you may have to do it many times in order to "hit the jackpot" as one says. An ovum has to be present in the woman's body at the time of ejaculation by the male or shortly thereafter (sperm can live for about twenty-four hours) and it also takes about the same amount of time for an egg to pass from the ovary down through the uterus and out through the vagina. This means that only during forty-eight hours, give or take, can a woman get pregnant at all. The "rhythm" method of birth control is based on this fact, but, as I noted in the chapter on methods of birth control, it is very unreliable since many experiences—emotional and physical—can upset a girl's rhythm and stray ova can escape off schedule.

"You only have intercourse to have a baby." By now you know that most people have intercourse to make love, and only now and then to make babies. Some religions have preached, however, that the pleasure of intercourse belongs only to those who leave themselves open to having a baby. If you believe this, it's a great pity, for some couples thus never get the pleasure they were promised since they are so burdened with pregnancy all the time. Intercourse has two functions: that of lovemaking and that of procreation, of which lovemaking is the more usual.

Here's a funny one for you: "Don't sit on damp ground or you won't be able to conceive a baby."

In fact, because of the tremendous emphasis in past historic time on "being fruitful and multiplying," a woman who didn't conceive resorted to all kinds of myths and magic to make herself conceive—these ranged from consulting witches to wearing talismen of one sort or another. One of the really cruel conception myths has it that the woman is at fault if she doesn't conceive. Many a woman has been cast aside in divorce because of the widespread belief in this fallacy—like the wives of Henry VIII. Actually, the "fault" may be either with the male or the female. He may have inactive sperm, or these may be insufficient in number or damaged from some childhood disease. She may have a blocked tube or a tubular spasm or scar tissue from an infection. Or the chemistry of her vaginal secretions may kill off the sperm of one man, but be entirely hospitable to those of another. Infertility has to be checked out in both partners to determine and eradicate possible causes.

Another cruel sexist conception myth is that the woman determines the sex of the child. In quite recent history a monarch was able to put aside his lawful and beloved wife because she gave him only female children. Actually, it is always the male who determines the sex of the child. A woman's body produces only X chromosomes, but a man produces both X and Y chromosomes. If fate has it that his X chromosome sperm merges with her ovum, a girl will result. If his Y chromosome sperm joins with her ovum, a boy will result. It is purely a matter of accident which sperm fertilizes her egg, though some specialists today feel that they can increase the chances of getting one sex or the other by having the mating take place at the beginning or end of her fertility period, since one seems to produce more girls and the other more boys.

Closely related to conception myths are those promising freedom from conception, such as:

If you don't want to get pregnant, don't kiss a boy.
Only French kissing gets you pregnant.
You won't get pregnant if you don't come to orgasm. (In fact, most of the world's babies have come into being when the woman, unfortunately, did not come to orgasm.)
If your hymen is intact, it forms a protective shield that keeps you from getting pregnant. (All hymens have perforations through which menstrual blood flows.)
You won't get pregnant if you don't fall in love.
You can get pregnant if you snuggle in bed with a man.
Pulling out is a method of birth control.

And here's one for laughs: A woman can be impregnated by a man who has ejaculated in a swimming pool, so always wear a bathing suit.

By now, all of you who have read through the book thus far know that all of these myths are "for the birds."

Sex and Aging

There are some peculiar myths about sex and age, such as:

No one over the age of fifty has intercourse. Young people find it hard to believe that older people enjoy sex, so this myth is easy for them to swallow. One recent study, however, showed that the vast majority of people over age sixty-five who had partners at all and who, at younger ages, enjoyed sex, still enjoyed sex. In fact, they continue to do so all their lives.

The myth that it's okay for an older man to marry a younger woman—it's a matter of status— but that for an older woman to marry a younger man, there has to be something wrong with her or her partner, is very pernicious. (If reason rather than tradition were functioning, this would be reversed. Given the cultural milieu we have known until now, a woman comes into sexual maturity later than a man and would be a much better sexual partner for him when he is twenty and she thirty. Also, women tend to live ten years longer than men, so both would have a better chance of companionship in old age. But I suppose it is asking too much for such a strongly ingrained tradition to be broken easily.)

If age and youth marry, it's sick. (Is it, now? What do you think?)

Religious Taboos

Religious myths and taboos are legion. You might start

with your own religion and make a list of myths you have grown up with. I wonder how many you believe emotionally, even though your head tells you they are nonsense.

"The eyes of God see everywhere and can even read your mind. If you have sexual thoughts, God will punish you."

I once knew a little girl who ran a low-grade fever for months. No medical doctor could discover its cause. One day her observant nursery school teacher heard her asking a bus driver if God were on his bus. When the driver said, "Yes, of course," the little girl refused to get on. The alert teacher made some further inquiries and soon found that the child was perpetually anxious about living in a world in which God was everywhere with his eyes so accusingly on her. The teacher had sense enough to send God back to his heavenly habitat (at least as far as the child was concerned) and forthwith, the child's fever disappeared like magic.

Religious taboo has been the greatest fear instiller of all time, because authority invokes even greater Authority with mystical powers to carry out terrible consequences. Fear of going to hell has terrorized many a child, and adult too, and the myths about enjoyment of sexual pleasure as the sure road to hell have created a living hell right here on earth. Perhaps the most revolutionary thing about the so-called sexual revolution is the realization that sexual energy can be the greatest force for good on earth when linked with love, and that "heaven" is at hand whenever lovers unite sexually and with love.

No religion has been absolutely free of the taboo method of "controlling" its followers, but many religions today are trying to make up for their past sin of "reign by terror" by being in the very forefront of those forces in our society attempting now to substitute truth for fiction. Enlightened church leaders are battling the old taboos that:

Sex is something you don't talk about.
Sex is dirty.
Sex is bad except in marriage.
Oral sex is perverted.
Homosexuals are queer.

And so on.

Homosexual Myths

And speaking of homosexuality, here is another group of myths that you may want to toss in the garbage can—I hope you will:

If you love someone of the same sex, you will never be able to love anyone of the opposite sex.

If you are homosexual, you are automatically a seducer of children (e.g., "I wouldn't let my boy be taught by a homosexual—he might induce him to become just like him." Sexual orientation has nothing to do with a person's character and trustworthiness).

Homosexuals can't be trusted in positions of responsibility.

Homosexuals are incapable of a sustained relationship.

All queers are men.

All—yes, *all*, are false.

Marriage and Pregnancy Myths

We come now to the marital myths and perhaps these are the most pernicious of all, since they encourage such a lot of assumptions which marital partners may have to take a lifetime of painful readjustment to undo. Such myths as these cause a lot of trouble:

I can change him after marriage, or she'll change once she's married.

If I love him enough his character will improve.

Once a couple is married, they never look twice at persons of the opposite sex unless there is something wrong with their relationship.

The man earns the living. The woman keeps the house and tends the children.

The man wears the pants and is boss of the show. He is head of the household. (Even income tax forms encourage this myth of "head of household" instead of encouraging "partnership relationships.")

Men should be free to come and go without question. Women should check with their husbands as to their comings and goings.

Men do the outdoor jobs around the home and women do the indoor ones.

Men should not be expected to have anything to do with the care of the babies.

Men decide when they shall have sex. "Man proposes: woman disposes."

The Women's Movement, along with multitudes of liberated men, are vigorously giving the lie to such myths, but it will probably be in your generation that they are completely dissipated.

I once did a bit of research on pregnancy myths, and you wouldn't believe the nonsense that women over the centuries have had to absorb. Nearly every crazy superstition that could cross people's minds has been offered up as a "do" or "don't" to pregnant females. Here are a few that some people still believe, though they are all untrue:

Don't raise your hands above your head or the baby will get strangled in his cord.

If you are frightened by something, it will leave a birthmark of its image on the baby.

Eat twice as much, for you are eating for two.

Don't have sex the last six weeks of pregnancy or you

will infect the birth canal. (Sometimes sex is forbidden to women who have a history of miscarriage. But sturdy, healthy women can generally enjoy intercourse until labor begins.)

Don't buy anything for the baby before it is born, or it may be born dead.

Don't pick a name for the baby until it is born (for the same reason).

Ask your mother—and your grandmother—to tell you the taboos and myths that they heard—and believed. Perhaps you will have a chance to laugh together.

16 ⑥ Reproduction in the Plant and Animal World

Stretching Your Sexual Imagination

Reproduction takes miraculous forms throughout plant and animal life, but with Walt Whitman we need to exclaim, "Why carp at a miracle. I see nothing but miracles."

You will have studied many of these miracles in your courses in botany, biology, and zoology, but let us look at some of these against the miracle of human life.

The most primitive way of reproduction is asexual; that is to say, where there are no sexual mechanisms as such. The living creature reproduces itself either by a process called *division* or by one called *budding*. In division the individual simply divides itself into two parts. In budding a swelling (or bud) develops, forming a new individual, and then separates.

Worms and starfish are examples of reproduction by division. Fresh water polyps are examples of reproduction by budding.

Another primitive form of reproduction is *sporulation*. In sporulation the organism develops special cells, called *spores*, which separate and become individuals; examples are ferns, mushrooms, and algae. If you look at ferns on their undersides, you can often find rows of little brown seedlike forms which are the *spores* and which may one day become ferns under the right conditions.

Division occurs but is helped along, rejuvenated, as it

were, by sexual reproduction (fertilization of a female individual by a male).

For example, you can clip off a piece of a sponge (a hydra) and you can obtain as many new individuals as you have made clips. But this process cannot go on forever. After a while they grow old and tired and remain inert—without energy to go on. In order for these individuals to regain the energy to reproduce once more, they need coupling with a male of the species.

Hermaphrodism is another form of reproduction. In its primitive manifestation the sperm cells and egg cells are produced simultaneously inside the same individual. Oysters are hermaphroditic—that is, part of the time the genital gland functions as a testicle and part of the time as an ovary. The old legend of eating oysters only during months in which there is an *r* in the name of that month is quite correct, for September through April the oyster is testicle (male) and good to eat. During May, June, July, and August the ovaries swell and fill with eggs, which turn whitish as they ripen. The oysters then are female and should not be eaten because fecundation takes place at this time. The spermatozoids which were born in the previous period now fertilize these eggs. Also, if you eat them at this time, you extinguish the bed.

Parthenogenesis is still another form of reproduction. It means "virgin birth" or reproduction without aid of the male. However, the term cannot be taken literally, for just as there is no indefinite division without coupling, there is no unlimited parthenogenesis without fertilization by the male.

The fertilized female produces several generations in which the power to reproduce continues. But then there comes a day when a very strange thing occurs. The female who has not encountered a male produces both males and females instead of simply females. These couple and once more produce females which are parthenogenetically endowed—that is, they reproduce without the aid of a male.

A good example of parthenogenesis (virgin birth) is the plant louse.

At some unspecified time in evolutionary history, the male organ specialized into the male individual. The female was the primitive or the primary organism. In many male organisms the male becomes little more than a sex organ itself. Certain mollusks, for example, attached by a stalk, cling as parasites to the coat of other mollusks. Then they become smaller, their nutritive function ceases, and the stalk takes root in the living substance. Only the male organ itself persists as an appendage to the female.

It is only among mammals and in certain groups of birds that the male is equal or superior to the female. One might almost say that the male, not having the job of reproduction, has more leisure to develop his other powers. The male and female at this point now differ nearly always.

If you look at a pair of blackbirds, you will see the male with black and shiny plumage while the female is a mousy gray. You would hardly guess that they belonged to the same species. The cock and the hen offer an even greater difference.

While hermaphrodism, as you may remember, demanded perfect resemblance of individuals, separation of the sexes leads to what is called *dimorphism*. Dimorphism simply means that the roles of male and female differ. Nature tends to pamper the males of some species and the females in others, seemingly without rhyme or reason.

The male hornet, for example, is notably smaller than the female. The female mason bee is far more beautiful than the male. While the male does nothing but loaf and bumble, she builds big domed clay nests where her offspring spend their larvae days. In addition, it is the female who is armed, carrying a sword which she can project when required.

Among mosquitoes the males live on flowers and tree trunks, but the females prick and suck the blood of mammals. The males go off on what almost looks like army maneuvers scouting for females. As soon as a male spots a female, he seizes her and disappears up into the air where their mating takes place.

Sexual differences (dimorphism) are generally unnoticeable in fish and reptiles, but they are very noticeable in most birds and mammals.

In birds the differences are usually of size, coloring, or quality of plumage and song. In mammals the differences are of size, shape, hair, beard, or horns.

Sometimes the female bird is finer and stronger, as in the falcon, but more often it is the male whom nature favors. He is the prince while she is the Cinderella before the appearance of the fairy godmother.

Among mammals she-bears and the she-kangaroos are smaller than the males. In all the deer tribes except the reindeer, only the male has horns.

The difference between cows and bulls is very considerable, between mares and stallions less so, between bitch and dog less still, and between female and male cats almost nil. Where differences are slight and are the direct consequence of the possession of sexual organs, the removal of those organs (called castration) tends to make the animal more like the female of the species.

This has been advanced as evidence of the theory of primitivity of the female. It follows that masculinity is an augmentation of the normal or the female, and in this sense is a "development."

Sexual differences among men and women vary. If you limit the differences to the nonsexual elements, there are very few. But if you include the sexual element, the differences are considerable.

Perhaps the outstanding nonsexual ones are that the adult female is generally smaller than the male and has less muscular force. She is rarely bald, but man generally has more hair over other areas of his body, except under the arms and over the pubis. She is normally fatter than the male and her skin is finer. Her skull capacity is about 15 percent less than his.

The coupling activities of sexual creatures are fascinating.

Whales, for example, heave over on their sides and join obliquely, belly to belly. The male organ is enormous—six to eight feet long and sixteen inches in circumference. The vulva (opening) of the female runs lengthwise on her body; near it is found the udder, which projects when she nurses her young. This udder has the capacity to eject so that when the whale cub hooks on by his lips, the milk is sent to him as from a pump.

Female seals and walruses turn over to receive the male. The female lies on her back and the male, who is much thicker and longer, covers her, propping himself on his arms. The coupling lasts seven or eight minutes.

The male tortoise climbs onto the female and installs himself there, clinging to her shell with the nails of his forefeet. There he remains for fifteen days, slowly introducing into her organs his long, round prong, ending in a pointed ball, pressing with all his strength the enormous clitoris of the female.

Sometimes crocodiles mate in the water and sometimes on land. When in the water they lie on their sides. When on land the female lies on her back.

When serpents couple, the two-pronged (bifurcated) penis penetrates the vagina as the bodies interlace coil on coil until their two heads are staring at each other—eye to eye over their stiffened coils—and there they remain for a long time.

Some male fish have penises and thus have true copulation with the female; for example, dogfish and sharks. The males grab the females, holding them with hooks; cartilagenous pieces penetrate the female opening and act as a slide to the penis.

The poor little female mole has quite a painful time when the male mates with her. Instead of a ready-made opening in her body, the male has practically to perform a surgical incision through her abdominal hide. Naturally she runs from him until she can burrow no more. Finally the male closes in and even while she is still burrowing to get away from him, he punctures her abdomen and introduces the sperm which will fertilize her.

Dogs too have something of a hard time with their mating. This is because the male's penis contains a hollow bone around which are the erectile tissues. These form a swelled ring around the base of the penis, and prevent the separation of the two animals after the act is accomplished. They appear to remain a long time uncomfortable in their inability to free themselves. The semen is not squirted into the female, but flows, drop by drop, down through the hollow bony tube and only gradually does the erectile tissue once again become flaccid, permitting the separation of dog and bitch.

Lobsters and crabs couple in a manner not unlike humans. The female pursued by the male is turned on her back, and then she permits him to stretch over her with his pincers wound in among her claws, almost as in an embrace.

With ants the female carries off the male on her back. He bends his abdomen into a bow toward her vulva. She flies with him, mounts him, then falls. He dies on the spot. The female gets up, returns to the nest and lays her eggs before dying herself.

Butterflies are very ardent. The males make voyages in quest of females. Frequently they fly coupled, the female carrying the male. Perhaps you have seen what looked like a butterfly with four wings. This was nothing more than two butterflies mating.

Birds have no erectile tissue; in other words, no penis. Coition (coupling) is by simple contact. The male mounts the female, holds her with feet and beak, their two openings pressing against each other, and the sperm of the male flows into the oviduct of the female. The female thus fertilized lays eggs which she keeps warm with her body until they hatch some days later.

The coupling of frogs lasts from fifteen to twenty days. The male clambers onto the female, encircles her with his arms, crosses his hands over her breast and embraces her thus, remaining immobile and insensible of all his surroundings. Nothing, literally nothing, can make him let go. The purpose of the embrace seems to be nothing more nor less than the excitation of her abdomen, which makes her release and deliver her eggs. As she does so the male sprays them with sperm as they pass out. She lays about a thousand at a time. These fertilized eggs develop first into polliwogs and then finally into frogs.

In fish there is rarely contact of male and female in the production of young. The object of male desire is not the female but the eggs she lays. He watches for those she is about to lay, and searches for those she has laid. He will deposit semen even on eggs he finds floating and whose mother he has never seen.

Salmon swim up rivers in troops, braving all manner of hardship, leaping dams and waterfalls, in their determination to find a quiet, sandy pool in a fresh water stream; unlike the adults who live in salt water, the young, to survive, must have fresh water. Each female troop has a female leader. Finally this leader determines exactly the right spot and lays her eggs, and then all the other females do likewise.

Trailing along behind come the males, with an old male as leader. When he comes to the eggs he drenches them with sperm, showing the young males how to do it. Then the young males imitate him and fecundate the same eggs. Thus these fish seem to have a sort of school in which the old initiate the young.

The young of creatures born through sexual fertilization are born alive; that is, *viviparous*. All mammals are viviparous, for example.

Human babies, then, being mammals, are born viviparous.

Other creatures are born from eggs laid by the mother and fertilized by the father. Sometimes these eggs are fertilized inside the mother, as in birds, and sometimes outside, as in most fish.

We could go on and on and on, staging an endlessly fascinating peep show of Nature's miraculous reproductive schemes. The scientists have given their long names to these; names that roll off your tongue like the chorus of a song in a foreign language. Maybe you will remember words like *parthenogenesis, hermaphrodism, budding, division, dimorphism*—and maybe you won't. It doesn't matter. What does matter is that you let your mind embrace the great, wide, wonderful world of sex in nature, and that you view your own sexuality against a background that stretches your imagination.

17 The Love Path

How to Get on It and Stay There

All of you have seen the film or know the story of *The Wizard of Oz*. It is one of the truest fairy tales ever written about "the love path." You will recall the Yellow Brick Road on the way to the Emerald City. The Emerald City, of course, is nothing more than the possibility of heaven on earth where people know how to relate lovingly to each other—and the Wizard (that magic dispenser of dreams fulfilled) is nothing more than each person's own potential for fulfilling his or her own goals.

Growth and Fulfillment

The Yellow Brick Road is plainly marked for those on their way to the Emerald City. If travelers are not distracted from the path, their way is unhampered and clear. But if they dally, say, into the "land of the poppies," they experience an immediate, though not too horrendous, reminder that they are off the path. If they pay no attention to a mild reminder, they encounter a tougher one—like the Wicked Witch of the West, and so on. And thus it is with the love path. Like the Yellow Brick Road it has guideposts. Here are some that you can watch for:

Start by asking yourself daily, "Have I done any act today that I would not like to have done to me?" And, as a corollary to that, "What have I done today that I *would* like to be the object of?"

These are very tough questions to address to yourself, and sometimes you may need the help of a friend to stimulate both your imagination and your honesty. But it doesn't take a very great stretch of imagination to get into the shoes of the recipients of your acts and to sense how they feel. If you don't like the feeling, you can be sure that your associates don't either. They like you less and less if you continue doing them. Knowing that they like you less and less, you end up liking yourself less and less. This, incidentally, is the basic cause of lack of self-confidence (notwithstanding all the stuff we read about people being victims of bad environments, overbearing parents, and so on).

Keep in mind that once you are beyond the diaper stage, once you've begun to face the world on your own as a free-thinking individual (and every one of you reading this book is well into that stage of development), you discover very promptly that you, and you alone, determine how confident, or how lacking in self-confidence you will be, despite what the world is like around you. And the major factor in that determination is your decision to practice what has come to be known as the Golden Rule. This rule is also the first guidepost on the love path (the Yellow Brick Road). It reads, "Do unto others as you would have them do unto you." And it simply means that before you do anything that others will be affected by, ask yourself if you would enjoy being the object of this action.

If your answer is uncertain or ambiguous, you may have to do some further thinking. Suppose you'd be perfectly happy to be the object of your action, but you know that someone else (perhaps your parents) may not share those feelings. In this area lie some of the toughest decisions that young persons have to make: action that feels right and good to you versus action that others claim "hurts them." When you are faced with such a dilemma, it may help to ask yourself this set of questions: "Am I really inflicting unnecessary pain on someone?" Or, "In my action (which is good for me) am I the involuntary instrument through which life itself inflicts pain on that other person?"

Let me explain: If a father says to his son, "If you insist on studying art instead of medicine, which your mother and I have counted on your doing, it will kill us. In fact, I believe your mother will have a heart attack." (This, by the way, is what I call the tyranny of weakness—blackmail, if you will.)

Now if the son goes ahead fulfilling his own destiny through the study of art, not medicine, and if, let us suppose, both mother and father suffer emotional disappointment because of it, we have to assume that the boy was not the cause of their pain, but merely the means through which they had to learn the painful lesson that no one, not even parents, can completely control another's life.

The boy, in this case, might feel very sad to have to act in a way contrary to his parents' dream for him, but he would certainly be involved in even greater suffering in the long run if he did not fulfill his own purposes.

On the other hand, if this same boy, not really caring about art as a profession, said to himself, "The one thing that will really get the old folks' dander up is to spoil their dream of me as a doctor. So I'll just let out that I plan to be an artist and watch them squirm! Then I'll really have something to bargain with them with," he, in turn, would be the blackmailer.

It is perfectly clear, of course, that there is a vast difference in motivation between these two acts. One, over time, could lead to growth of all the members of the family. The other, over time, could tear the family apart.

So ask yourself, as you pursue your own development, "Is the path I am on important to my growth and fulfillment? Will it hurt? Is there any way I can avoid the hurt? And am I an instrument or a cause?" If you are still in doubt, you can check with some other loving, responsible adults (your own self-chosen role models) as to the possible and probable results of proposed action that is at variance with your parents' wishes.

A Loving Touch

We have already talked a lot about everyone's need for affectionate touch, but let's acknowledge that need again now. We all know that we touch that which we like. Even our pets sense this and rub against our legs asking for a friendly pat. Many a person (male and female) has experienced the melting away of anger tensions, worry tensions, and tension of any origin by the simple expedient of being held in someone's loving arms.

So the guidepost on the Yellow Brick Road is, "Youth is a good time to gain practice and skill in recognizing the need for touch in those you love, and asking for it when you need it." Dare to offer it. You may occasionally suffer a rebuff, but this is something you can learn to handle. Every adult suffers rebuffs in many areas of life and simply has to acquire greater and greater skill in recognizing when and under what circumstances his or her actions will be acceptable. Each time you dare to risk offering your gift of touch you are increasing your own capacity to perceive accurately. If you are timid, you can always inquire. For example, you can ask either your mother or your lover, with equal confidence, "Would you like a back rub?" There are very few persons I know who can resist such an offer.

Sometimes just a good-bye hug for dad or mom can make their day—even though it may seem to you that they have given up such indulgences with you long ago. A pat on little sister's head, a friendly arm around grandma's shoulder with a quickie massage of her stiffening neck, are gestures that require so little of your time and may be experienced by those who receive them as a renewal of life itself.

And how do you tell your parents that you, too, would like a little physical affection? I think you simply say to them that your back is hungry for one of those good-night rubs that dad used to give you when you were a little fellow. And what mother could resist your letting her know that you'd like your head in her lap while she stroked it as both of you were watching TV. Even little sister will try to rub your neck after you've stroked hers—especially if you make a lot of approving noises that let her know how good she makes you feel.

The overall result of such loving touch is a flow of love that moves between you and nourishes all of you.

Work, Sharing and Caring

A third guidepost on the love path has to do with work. We share most of our lives with those with whom we work. Our fellow workers are our closest companions throughout our waking days. Even outside of the jobs by which we earn our living, we still share work with those with whom we live. Even lovers, maybe especially lovers, must share work loads. If each carries his or her agreed-upon portion cheerfully, deep feelings of respect and affection result. But if one slacks off, shifting the burden onto another, or does his or her job grumpily, the reverse occurs. Maybe not just at first (such as in the infatuation stage of a new love), but surely, insidiously, increasingly over time, resentment replaces love and trust.

One of the rather interesting findings that have come out of a study of the communes in this country (and also of the alternate life-style marriages) has been that no able-bodied person who doesn't do his or her share of the work can be endured for long in a commune. The same could be said of families. In a household where most of the chores are performed by the adults, with little or no participation by the children, there soon grows up hidden resentment (sometimes not so hidden). These are expressed as, "You ought to be grateful. Can't you see that we slave our lives away for you kids, and the very least you can do is show your gratitude (by accepting our suggestions and doing exactly as we say)." In other words, there develops a hidden agenda when there is a disparity of responsible contribution between the members of a close-knit group. There is no way, I repeat, *no way* that one person can always be the "given-to" and another always be the "giver" and not create a backlog of resentment. The most devoted mother or father or big brother or sister is sometimes going to explode—and rightfully. The Yellow Brick Road requires that work loads be shared, each member doing what he or she is capable of on behalf of the common good.

Somewhat related to work, but transcending it in its power to create good feelings, is the observance of small acts of personal service that make another person's life more pleasureful. Not a necessary, vital job, counted on by the community, not an assigned task for which you will be blamed if you forget to do it, but that extra expenditure of effort on your part that is *not* counted on—like bringing your mother breakfast in bed, offering to take the kinks out of dad's back with a back rub, reading to baby brother, writing your grandmother a note, helping your friend with a tough bit of homework, baking a batch of cookies for the family, or sharpening the kitchen knives—and on and on and on. A caring eye can see so much that, when implemented by such small acts, can bring joy into the lives of others. An uncaring eye is blind to the opportunities at hand for loving action. Then, of course, the owner of that "blind" eye complains that "nobody loves me."

Over the years I have learned to doubt the motivations of those who say, "I have so much love to give—why is it that no one seeks me out to receive the rich gifts I hold in my hands?"

Actually, such a person is not saying, "I want to give," but rather, "I want to get." I want to swap service for love. I want a guarantee, with interest, on my investment.

On the other hand, the person who finds a lot to give and gives it freely never has occasion to worry if he or she is loved in return. Such persons are so busy with the joy of giving and the fun of building a loving atmosphere that the notion of repayment is outside the realm of expectation. They are probably basking in the love that surely does come their way as they travel the road to the Emerald City.

Perhaps a word here may be helpful about the difference between *giving* and *swapping*. Very few of us give without an anticipation of getting something in return. What we do then is swap, not give. Now there is nothing intrinsically wrong with fair trading, as long as the parties to the deal have agreed upon the terms. These are legitimate trades. The harmful swaps are those that masquerade as gifts. These carry an unknown, unspecified, non-agreed-upon price tag, and if payment isn't rendered as anticipated, a great howl goes up. For example: "If I do the dishes every night (which I hate), I expect you to mow the lawn" (though I don't tell you about this). When you don't mow the lawn I assume that you don't love me.

I am sorry to say that parents indulge in this a lot. So do lovers. They make assumptions based on such ersatz giving and then find themselves wallowing in self-pity when they are disappointed in their expectations. Many conclude that "acts of kindness don't pay."

Actually, gifts of love always pay the giver because his or her satisfaction lies in the giving and especially in the expressed pleasure of the receiver. Now, if such a giving person's life gets out of balance through overdoing the giving and never paying attention to personal needs, he or she may end up feeling starved and will have to get nourishment from somewhere. However, he (or she) had best not expect, as a matter of course, that the nourishment will all come from the one to whom one has given. Generally, if we give to life we are likely to get back from life, but there is no guarantee of an even trade between the individuals involved—except by explicit arrangement.

So give for the joy of it without expectation of return, for giving is fun in itself. But also make reasonable swaps with those you love for the fulfillment of your own needs and make them by mutual agreement.

Appreciation

A fourth guidepost reads—in large letters—*appreciation*. One thing that made my own marriage sing for me was my husband's consistent generosity with appreciation and praise. Not a day in all our thirty-seven years of marriage did he neglect to find some positive thing, no matter how trivial, to tell me about myself. The other side of that same coin was that he never criticized, unless I asked for it or unless we mutually agreed to a "growth session," usually preceded by, "Are you in a mood to hear suggestions?"

This kind of consideration did generate, and always does generate, loving responses, and it minimizes resistance to change.

Many persons, when they are discontented, blow off steam around other people—usually loved ones—and then, quite naturally, get negative responses. Then they conclude mistakenly that these people no longer are their friends and that angry feelings are wrong or bad.

It is probably a good thing to let off steam from time to time, but the benefits are negligible if you fly off the handle at someone with whom the love relationship is important. You may feel great relief from unloading your anger, but the person "dumped on" feels awful, and may become unpleasantly defensive. It may then take a good deal of time and effort for you to reestablish a good flow of feeling between you again.

If anger release is in order, and it often is, then try pounding a couch, screaming into the wind (or a pillow), biting on a towel, running around the block, or playing a vigorous game of tennis, making sure you name the object of anger each time you hit the ball. Thus no one gets hurt while your anger tension is letting go, and later your good brain, freed of tension, will be able to go to work to solve the problem that caused the trouble in the first place (and without having to soothe hurt feelings first).

As you have probably gathered by now, one of the penalties of held-onto anger is that it does tend to paralyze your capacity to think, since most of your energy is going into tensing anger muscles to keep from letting go aggressively which, theoretically, at least, we don't do in this so-called civilized world. So pretty soon you may either explode or implode. If you "explode" you are likely to hurt someone. If you "implode" you may hurt yourself by getting ulcers, temporal-mandibular joint dysfunctions, or bursitis, for example. The obvious answer is to find a safe way to let your tense muscles move so that no one will be hurt and nothing of value will be broken. If actual damage does occur you will find that the guilt burden is just too much to bear, and then a rather vicious thing may happen. Since no one can live very long with guilt, you may try to lay blame on someone else, or you may try to prove that the other fellow provoked the action. "He deserves what I gave him," you tell yourself. The resulting atmosphere is not loving. On the other hand, if you release tension by harmless physical activity, you may then be relaxed enough to consider a more effective approach to the anger-provoking situation. For example, you may tell your friend that you want to talk to him (or her) about something that you are reacting to in a negative way.

At this point, there is something else that is very important in establishing a loving atmosphere. I mentioned it briefly in Chapter 8 "Sex and Your Family," but it should be noted again. Never say to a friend, "You make me angry" (sad, afraid, etc.). Rather, take responsibility for your own feelings by saying, "I feel angry when you—" (whatever it is your friend does that you don't like).

This approach doesn't put your friend on the defensive—doesn't lay a guilt trip. Your friend can then get over on your side and look at the problem, rather than be forced to defend him- or herself. A game we play in camp, which helps mutual understanding, goes like this. Take a partner you know well (and would like to know better). Ask this partner to do the following:

"Tell me something that you like about me."

"Tell me something that you think we agree on."

"Tell me something that you think I should know about you."

The friend has five minutes to follow these directions while the requester sits quietly listening, with no interruption whatsoever. It is best if the listener sits face-to-face with his or her partner, with hands open (not clenched) and with a facial expression of attentive openness.

At the end of five minutes, the timekeeper calls time, and the listener simply says, "Thank you." No comments, no argument, defense, or apology. Just "Thank you" (for the communication).

Obviously, the first and second requests are fun to do and they put the listener in a mood to "hear" the third, which is sometimes not so easy to absorb. For this third request gives the speaker a chance to let his or her partner really understand more about himself or herself and to communicate what the other is doing (or not doing) that is bothersome or pain-giving. Here again, when imparting such knowledge, be very careful not to lay a guilt trip on the listener. For example, you might say, "I think you should know about me that I get very nervous when you are late for an appointment." Not, "You make me nervous by being late."

From the first expression, a person can "hear" about his (or her) failings because the focus is on the reactions of the other fellow. The listener can then choose what he or she wants to do about the behavior. But hearing "You make me," the listener usually becomes defensive and closes up.

A game such as this, when played for an hour or two, each taking five-minute turns to answer the requests (always the same requests), begins to open up deeper levels of communication against a background of deeper appreciation. In other words, partners can come away from such an experience loving each other more.

Another game that increases capacity for appreciation is the exercise of giving a friend a compliment. This is played as follows: A group of friends sit in a circle. One person starts off by turning to the neighbor on the left and telling that person something that he (she) likes about him (her). This part is relatively easy. Next comes the hard part. The one receiving the compliment must respond to it in such a way as to make the giver pleased and happy to have offered this gift of praise.

Long before everyone in the circle has completed their turn, the atmosphere in the room will exude good feelings. Furthermore, friends cease to be afraid to give and receive the wonderful nourishment of praise.

The Divine Spark

A fifth guidepost on the Yellow Brick Road is optimism.

As you may suspect, optimism is the gift of positive expectation. When someone expects the best from you, you tend to be better, to do better, and to give more whole-heartedly of yourself.

Of course you are acquainted with the definition of the optimist as one who sees the edible part of a doughnut and the pessimist as one who sees the hole. Corny as this definition may be, it is close to the truth. Perhaps some of you have seen the play, *The Rainmaker*, in which a dreary, rain-starved, love-starved farm community was transformed almost overnight by a visiting hobo who spread hope and faith. Tagore defined faith as "the bird that feels the light and sings when the dawn is yet dark." It is such a song that quickens our hearts and gives rise to that extra spurt of energy that often enough does indeed transform dreams into realities.

I am not suggesting that you develop the habit of leading yourself or others down the primrose path of dreams that hold no possibility of fulfillment. That would be cruel indeed. But develop an attitude of mind that is open to the best projectable outcome of any situation and bend your efforts to produce it.

Incidentally, such an attitude is the only one I know that holds the key to human change for the better. A wise psychiatrist under whom I trained practiced this regularly. His thesis was that you can only build from those fragments of the divine spark that are alive in any given individual. Find these, encourage them, and soon they will warm and permeate larger and larger areas of the personality. This approach to health, he found, worked better than bringing the "sick" areas of a personality to light and dwelling on them. This is not to say that a gardener can develop a fine garden without doing a job of weeding now and then. But the primary job is encouraging and tending the plants and nourishing the soil.

In your own human relationships you might enjoy observing your associates with your *eyes* focused on what you *like* about them, and then finding some way to communicate these positive discoveries.

Bibliotherapy

A sixth guidepost reads *bibliotherapy*—which simply means "the inspiration and healing power of books," particularly the reading of love stories. Novels, biographies, autobiographies offer a rich treasure trove of guidance, and they expand your concept of what love is all about: Love between man and man, love between man and God, love between man and woman, woman and woman, parents and children, master and pet, devotion to causes, countries, principles, and love of work.

In the Bibliography, I have listed just a few of the tales that have shaped my own life, along with some that my friends have reported have shaped theirs. You could make your own list and ask your friends to share theirs with you. I might add that a wonderful defense against disillusion and depression is to have a novel stashed beside your bed (ready for instant reading in time of need). Then, when you're feeling low or dispirited or doubtful that there is any true love at all left in the world, just pick the book up and nourish yourself with it. Chances are, as you lose yourself in another's love, you will come back to your own life with a new look at the dimensions of love—along with some hunches as to where and how to find it.

Humor

The seventh guidepost is *humor*. Whenever I've asked anyone to write down the qualifications that they would want their "dream prince" or "dream princess" to have, the phrase *a sense of humor* regularly appears near the top of the list.

A sense of humor doesn't mean that you have to be "funny" (though when I was a teenager I used to think it did and I was intensely envious of my brother's capacity to make people laugh). It does mean, however, that you can't take yourself so seriously that you don't see the funny side of your own behavior or of life around you. Actually, when you meditate about it at all, there is something ridiculously amusing about the ways the peoples of the world go about their daily living. If you allowed yourself the leisure to consider these, you'd have a chuckle in your throat a good deal of the time. You'd be a sage, in fact. If you can react to your disappointments, not only with appropriate anger, grief, or frustration, but also with a laugh, you can heal yourself of permanent scarring. Loving couples do this regularly, as part and parcel of their partnership. In so doing they add years of health to their life spans and give each other new links to the bridge on which one can reach the other.

Trust

A final major guidepost reads *trust* (written large). I suppose that it goes without saying that all love is based on trust. But maybe this had better be said again emphatically, for often we accept this thesis without regard for its full implications.

Let's say it another way: Love corrodes and disappears in the absence of trust.

This fact does not mean that a person has to be fully trustworthy in every aspect of his or her being to be loved and loving. This isn't so, for all of us are mortal, and being mortal are imperfect, and thus have spots of untrustworthiness. However, if the thrust of our lives is toward truth, the chances are that we won't let down our loved ones in any substantial way. And if, perchance, we do so without intention, we will bend every effort to rectify our mistakes.

In talking about guideposts leading toward the Emerald City, I haven't mentioned at all the danger signals leading away from it, such as, "Take this turnoff at your own risk," or "Follow this trail and you end up in the slough of despair." Actually, there are very few of these, but there are at least four that you should know about, for they are guaranteed to lead you straight into the bogs of depression and isolation. Also, each and every one of them is a love killer.

Their names are jealousy, possessiveness, perfectionism, and the need to control others.

Before mankind knew better, there was a tendency to mask these as virtues. For example, "jealousy is a sign of love." It is not, of course, for jealousy is really a reflection of a person's sense of inadequacy and insecurity; through jealous behavior he or she tries to place limitations on your actions to humor his or her own weakness.

Whenever any of us are limited from outgoing, friendly action toward others, we feel caged and begin to chafe at unnecessary restrictions. After a while our love for the jailer diminishes.

Love itself is always *liberating*.

A possessive person is confining. None of us is or can be owned by another, so we necessarily feel as if our wings were clipped when someone (even a loved someone) tries to "own" us. Furthermore, the moment there is a master-slave relationship between any two persons, what really happens is that there are two slaves.

Since love operates only in an atmosphere of freedom, love soon withers and dies in the opposite atmosphere, namely, slavery.

A perfectionist is one who can never be satisfied because there is no such thing as perfection. So whatever you do to please him (or her), you will never succeed in your effort. After a while this is so discouraging that you will cease trying, and love itself will then disappear.

A person who must control others, including you, is operating what may be called "the forcing current."

Most of us tend to resist force, for it interferes with our own natural life patterns, and no one likes to "have a trip laid on them." We prefer to be self-determining. So when someone comes along who consistently tells us what to do and how to do it, we begin to withdraw and eventually to dislike that person.

There is a saying that when force walks in the door, love flies out the window.

Most adults who recognize the nasty effects of the "love killers" try hard to rid themselves of these characteristics.

It is very hard indeed. In fact, you may discover that it can be a lifetime job, but every time you succeed in rolling away such an obstruction, you will feel better about yourself and you will also feel the good firm earth of the love path beneath your feet.

As I sit here writing this last page of *Sex, with Love*, I see you, the youth of our country, striding joyously down the love path—unoppressed by the bogeys of ignorance with which your parents struggled. I see you blossoming and blooming as you revel in your God-given pleasure senses. And I see you using these responsibly and lovingly.

If you are frustrated by the slow way the adult world about you moves in applying what it knows to the way it behaves emotionally toward your wonderful sexuality, try to remember that it grew up with very different information.

It was, in fact, only twenty-five years ago that a courageous little band of researchers tried to probe such a simple unknown as the dimensions of erotic desire. By then it was known that infants were born sexual beings, but no scientist had established how late in the life span of humans sexual desire continued. The "going" assumption was that it ended with menopause for women and with a phenomenon akin to menopause for men. So these researchers turned to one of their members, a lively old lady in her late seventies, and asked, "When does sexual desire stop?"

With her eyes twinkling, she answered, "I'll let you know."

Today we know beyond all doubt that sex is from birth to death. It remains only for us to rejoice in the knowledge and to become artists in its use.

Appendix I

How to Find Professional Help:
A Note About Shrinks and Growers

If you decide to seek help for a problem you are having about sexuality, about communicating with others, or about low self-image, how do you begin to "shop" for a counselor or therapist? Yes, it is okay to look around a bit until you find a human being you can relate to in a way that feels good to you. What you want to find is not someone who will try to "shrink" you, but someone who will help you grow and expand your understanding.

Very often it is the trust that builds between you and a professional "grower" that is the most healing and expanding thing: the faith that *you* can learn to handle your own problems (along with some practical suggestions) rather than a bunch of "shoulds" and "oughts."

Above all, know that you don't have to be sick or crazy to seek counseling. Though there are some old-fashioned ethics that say "you're supposed to be able to solve all your own problems by yourself," it is (thank heaven) becoming more and more okay to see a professional when your problems feel too big or the way too unknown for you to handle without guidance or consultation. Remember, too, that we *all* have problems and that doesn't make us all "sick." It's how we choose to cope with the problems we have that may make or break us as happy, productive human beings.

Professional help falls into several categories (one counselor may have several of these titles):

Psychiatrists: These are M.D.s, trained especially to deal with mentally and emotionally sick people, often in a hospital setting.

Psychoanalysts: These are generally M.D.s (but not always)

163

who do long-term therapy (several times a week) for a year or more. You talk (or "free-associate") aloud, and they are trained to give very little feedback, allowing you to gradually discover for yourself the emotional forces at work in your life.

School Psychologists: These are often trained to give and interpret personality tests, like those multiple-choice exams you have in school, or they may be trained in various kinds of therapy. Some may specialize in working with families, young people, and so forth. Many psychologists are helpful problem solvers.

Psychotherapists: These are sometimes psychologists, sometimes psychiatrists, and sometimes professionals trained in some special form of action therapy designed to help you work through emotional blocks and relationship problems. Sex therapists, for instance, are especially trained to help you deal with physical, emotional, and relationship issues around your sexuality.

Counselors: These may be ministers, school counselors, nurses, Planned Parenthood or family planning persons, workers in youth centers, Rape Crisis centers, and abortion clinics. They may be paid or volunteer. They are trained to do "short-term" counseling (one or two times), and can be helpful in referring you to a psychotherapist if your problem looks like it's going to take more than a few sessions.

There are ways that you yourself can find a counselor or therapist who will help you solve your particular problems.

You can talk with your school nurse, school counselor, pastor, doctor, teacher, or family planning or Planned Parenthood clinic—any adult who works with young people and whom you feel you can trust. This person may be directly helpful to you or may be able to steer you to someone who can be.

If you draw a blank here, you can write to the American Association of Marriage and Family Counselors, 225 Yale Avenue, Claremont, California 91711, or to the American Association of Sex Educators and Counselors and Therapists, 5010 Wisconsin Avenue, N.W., Suite 304, Washington, D.C. 20016, asking "who is a trained, sympathetic counselor or therapist in my area who can help me?" (Be sure to state your age.) Also, both organizations publish directories.

Even though it may be scary for you to admit to yourself and others that you have a problem, that admission is often a giant step toward real growth and maturity. And you may be surprised to find, as you look around, that you're not the *only one* with "your" problem.

Appendix II

Community Resources

(Look for local listings in the White or
Yellow Pages of your Telephone Book)

Problem	Resources
Need for information or help with gynecological examination, Pap smear, birth control, pregnancy test, unwanted pregnancy, abortion	Family Planning Planned Parenthood Women's Centers Women's Health Clinics National Organization for Women
Need for information or help with V.D.	National V.D. Hot-Line (Operation Venus)—telephone toll free 1—800—272—2577 Planned Parenthood Your state's Division of Public Health, V.D. Division, or Department of Communicable Diseases, or a local V.D. clinic. Clinics are often in a hospital and might be called "skin clinic" or "L" clinic (L stands for luctic—another name for syphilis).
If you have been raped or want help for someone who	Rape Crisis Centers

(continued)

Problem	Resources
has been raped. Need for information or help with rape crisis.	
Need for sex counseling	Sex Counselors Sex Therapists Write: American Association of Sex Educators and Counselors and Therapists (AASECT), 5010 Wisconsin Ave., N.W., Suite 304, Washington, D.C. 20016, for professionals in your area or send for their directory ($3.00).
Need for counseling in matters of love relationships	Write: American Association of Marriage and Family Counselors (AAMFC), 225 Yale Avenue, Claremont, California 91711, for professionals in your area.
Need for help with family crisis or other relationship crisis	Women's Centers Teen Centers Hot Lines Family Centers Ministers, Priests, Rabbis. Many are trained pastoral counselors who can either help you or refer you to someone who can. Many churches and synagogues have youth centers.

Books That List Additional Resources

Boston Women's Health Care Collective, *Our Bodies, Ourselves* (New York: Simon and Schuster, rev. ed., 1976).

Braun, Saul, ed., *The Catalog of Sexual Consciousness* (New York: Grove Press, 1975).

Madduk, Hilary, *Menstruation* (New York: Tobey Publishing, 1975).

Annotated Bibliography

Below you will find listed some books that I have found useful.

Of course these are only a sampling of the wealth awaiting you. I encourage you to look both in your library and in your local bookstores for these and other books of interest to you. Many of them are in paperback and you may want to own them. Your bookstore will probably be happy to order any of them for you. Since many of these books are new and some are published by small presses, do not be surprised if your local library does not have them all in stock. If you do not find the title listed in the card catalog you can request the librarian to order it. Some librarians are very responsive to such requests.

Caring for Your Body

Downing, George, *The Massage Book* (New York: Random House, 1972).

> For anyone who wants to learn how to massage with skill and love.

Samuels, Mike, and Hal Bennett, *The Well Body Book* (New York: Random House/Bookworks, 1973).

> How to be your own doctor without replacing your physician—total body care for males and females.

Boston Women's Health Care Collective, *Our Bodies, Ourselves* (New York: Simon and Schuster, rev. ed., 1976).

> Now the classic resource book on health care for women —and the best I know. Includes chapters on sexuality, reproduction, birth control, V.D., rape, self-defense, abortion, pregnancy.

Dodson, Betty, "Liberating Masturbation," 1974 (Bodysex Designs, P.O. Box 1933, New York, N.Y. 10001).

> Beautifully illustrated booklet to help you appreciate a woman's genitalia.

169

Wallace, Jane, *Masturbation: A Woman's Handbook* (Brooklyn: Side Hill Press).

Stories told by real women about what it's like to give themselves sexual pleasure.

You and Your Family

Ogden, Gina, and Anne Zevin, *When a Family Needs Therapy* (Boston: Beacon Press, 1976).

A delightful guide to understanding how you and your family can communicate and solve problems and have fun together.

Satir, Virginia, *Peoplemaking*, paperback edition (Palo Alto: Science and Behavior Books, 1975).

How your family acts and some things to do about that. Both of the above are written in plain language for families rather than for therapists.

Sex and Loving

Hamilton, Eleanor, *Sex Before Marriage* (New York: Bantam Press [for paperback edition], 1969), or write the author: Eleanor Hamilton, Ph.D., Hamilton School, Inc., Sheffield, Mass. 01257.

A guide for sex with love for ages 16 and up.

Bowan, Elisa, *How Can I Show That I Love You?* (Celestia Arts Publishing, 231 Adrean Road, Millbrae, Calif. 94030, 1972).

Sex Resource Books Compiled for Adults

Braun, Saul, ed., *Catalogue of Sexual Consciousness* (New York: Grove Press, 1975).

A resource catalog that provides a selection of materials on human sexuality.

Hite, Shere, *The Hite Report* (New York: Macmillan, 1976).

Three thousand women describe in their own words their most intimate feelings about sex.

The Yes Book of Sex (Multi-Media Resource Center, 540 Powell St., San Francisco, Calif. 94102).

The Multi-Media Resource Center is a research, production, and distribution center of films, tapes, pamphlets and books about human sexuality. I advise you to send for their complete catalog.

Understanding Adolescence

Gordon, Sol, *You* (New York: Quadrangle: The New York Times Book Company, 1975).

Especially written for teenagers. Deals with all aspects of growing up, in current language; includes comic book illustrations. Outrageous and kids love it.

Boys and Sex

Pomeroy, Wardell, *Boys and Sex* (New York: Delacorte Press, 1968).

Pomeroy, Wardell, *Girls and Sex* (New York: Delacorte Press, 1969).

Very informative sound philosophy—though somewhat dated—written by a pioneer in the sex field.

Birth

Leboyer, Frederick, *Birth Without Violence* (New York: Knopf, 1975).

Tender and beautiful. Very appealing pictorial presentation of birth at its best.

Rape

Brownmiller, Susan, *Against Our Will* (New York: Simon and Schuster, 1975 [now in paperback]).

The best book about rape that I know.

Novels and Others

Buck, Pearl, *The Good Earth* (New York: Pocket Books, 1975).

Gibran, Kahlil, *The Broken Wings* (New York: Bantam, 1968).

Hall, Radclyffe, *The Well of Loneliness* (New York: Pocket Books, 1975).

Hawthorne, Nathaniel, *The Scarlet Letter* (New York: Harper & Row, 1970).

Hemingway, Ernest, *A Farewell to Arms* (New York: Scribner & Sons, 1967).

Hemingway, Ernest, *For Whom the Bell Tolls* (New York: Scribner & Sons, 1940).

Hudson, William H., *Green Mansions* (New York: AMSCO School Publications, 1970).

Huxley, Aldous, *Island* (New York: Harper & Row, paperback, 1972).

Lawrence, D. H., *Lady Chatterley's Lover* (New York: Grove Press, 1969).

Lawrence, D. H., *The Man Who Died*, bound with *Saint Mawr* (New York: Random House, 1959).

Longfellow, Henry Wadsworth, *Evangeline* (New York: Avon Books).

Michener, James, *Sayonara* (New York: Fawcett World Books, 1976).

Michener, James, *Fires of Spring* (New York: Fawcett World Books, 1976).

Morgan, Claire, *The Price of Salt* (New York: Arno Press, 1975).

Stephens, James, *The Crock of Gold* (New York: Macmillan, Inc., 1960).

Undset, Sigrid, *Kristin Lavransdatter* (New York: Alfred A. Knopf, Inc., 1951).

Wertenbaker, Lael Tucker, *Death of a Man* (Boston: Beacon Press, 1974).

Wilder, Thornton, *Woman of Andros* (New York: Avon Books, 1975).

Wright, Austin T., *Islandia* (New York: ArnoPress, 1971).

Index

Incest: 91-92
Infertility: 130-131
Intercourse: 21; fear of, 28-29;
inadvisability of, 38; positions for,
25-26; requirements for success,
30-31
I.U.D.: 95

J

Jealousy: 159
Joy (William Schutz): 49

K

Kinsey, Dr. Alfred: 65
Kissing good night: 52

L

Labia majora: 15
Labia minora: 15
Language, influential: 78-79
Lobsters, coupling activity of: 142
"Love killers": 159-160
Love versus sexual pressure: 50-51
Loving touch: 148-149
Lubricants, for intercourse: 24; for
masturbation, 34

M

Mace gun: 85
Male affection: 67
Mammals: 144
Marijuana: 51; and sex, myth, 127
Marriage myths: 134-135
Massage: 41; technique of, 56-57
The Massage Book (George Down-
ing): 57
Masturbation: 3, 32, 80; and
menstrual cramps, 121; as substi-
tute, 35-36; extending, 35;
mutual, 39; myths, 122-123;
need for, 36-37
Maternity center: 112
Meeting people: 45-46
Menopause: 18-19

Menstruation: 2-5, 8; myths of,
120-122
Mood shifts: 4
Moles, coupling activity of: 142
Monilia: 104, communicability of,
126-127
Morning-After Pill: 99-100

N

Natural childbirth: 112
Need to control others: 160
Nocturnal emission: 8
Noncoital petting to orgasm: 39-41
Nuclear family: 61

O

Optimism, gift of: 155-157
Orgasm: 3, 21; male, 8, 13, 24;
myths of, 128-129
Ovaries: 14
Ovulation: 2, 14
Ovum: 2, 14

P

Pain, in intercourse: 26
Parent-child sexuality: 76
Parental deprivation: 64
Parents: discussions with, 73-76;
living with affectionately, 148-
151
Paresis: 102
Parthenogenesis: 138
Peeping Tom: 88
Penicillin: 101-102
Penis: size of, 27; myths, 124-125
Perfectionism, and love: 159
Pessimist: 156
Petting, mutual: 32; to orgasm, 39
Phallic worship: 23
Physical maturity: 72
Pill, the: 94-95
Pituitary gland: 18
Poetry: 9
Police and rape: 86
Population explosion: 93